HOW TO FIND
WORK WHEN
YOU'RE OVER

More related titles

Learning to Counsel
Develop the skills you need to counsel others

'A very easy to read, easy to understand book which gives practical help and information on what counselling involves at all levels...' – Amazon reader review

Passing Psychometric Tests
Know what to expect and get the job you want

'A very good aid for those who might find themselves facing a psychometric questionnaire.' – *Irish Examiner*

'An insightful book.' – *The Guardian*

Returning to Work
A guide to re-entering the job market

'An absolute must for anyone who feels they wish to discover their potential and begin a new phase of life ... it helps with self-evaulation to define the most suitable type of job, then demonstrates the best ways to overcome the barriers that might block the opportunity to continue a career or start anew.' Institute of Management

Touch Typing in Ten Hours
Spend a few hours now and gain a valuable skill for life

'It works! Even if you are a two-fingered, search-and-hunt, typist you can learn to touch type if you follow the ten one-hour exercises.' – *Writers' News*

howtobooks

Please send for a free copy of the latest catalogue:

How To Books
3 Newtec Place, Magdalen Road,
Oxford OX4 1RE, United Kingdom
email: info@howtobooks.co.uk
http://www.howtobooks.co.uk

HOW TO FIND
WORK WHEN
YOU'RE OVER

*Make the most of your maturity
and experience to find the right job*

JACKIE SHERMAN

howto**books**

Published by How To Books Ltd,
3 Newtec Place, Magdalen Road,
Oxford OX4 1RE, United Kingdom.
Tel: (01865) 793806. Fax: (01865) 248780.
email: info@howtobooks.co.uk
http://www.howtobooks.co.uk

British Library Cataloguing in Publication Data
A catalogue record for this book is available from the British
Library

Cover design by Baseline Arts Ltd, Oxford
Produced for How To Books by Deer Park Productions, Tavistock
Typeset by PDQ Typesetting, Newcastle-under-Lyme
Printed and bound by Cromwell Press, Trowbridge, Wiltshire

NOTE: The material contained in this book is set out in good
faith for general guidance and no liability can be accepted
for loss or expense incurred as a result of relying in particular
circumstances on statements made in the book. The laws and
regulations are complex and liable to change, and readers should
check the current position with the relevant authorities before
making personal arrangements.

Contents

1. Introduction   **1**
   Changes to the current position   2
   Computers and job search   4
   Organising your job search   6

2. Knowing What You Could Do   **8**
   What makes a good job?   9
   Working conditions   10
   Skills and abilities   11
   Improving yourself   21
   Disabilities   23
   Interest and motivation   24
   Types of work   25
   Websites for older people   28
   Careers advice   28
   Which job to choose   29
   Summary   30

3. Finding Vacancies   **32**
   How you hear of a job   32
   The role of the Internet   33
   Local newspapers   34
   National press   35
   Magazines and journals   36
   Shop windows   38
   Home working   38
   Calling in person   39
   Agencies   39
   Vacancy websites   40
   Companies online   43
   Job centres   44
   Speculative approaches   45
   Networking   46
   Advertising yourself   47
   Summary   48

4.	**Is the Job Right for You?**	**50**
	Analyse the advert	50
	Finding out more	53
	Decision time	56
	Summary	56
5.	**Applying in Writing**	**57**
	What employers look for	57
	Empty statements	58
	Providing the evidence	60
	Follow the instructions	62
	Word-processing	64
	Sending off for details	65
	Covering letters	68
	References	74
	Speculative letters	76
	Summary	81
6.	**Producing a CV**	**82**
	What it is not	82
	Appearance	83
	Desktop publishing	84
	Types of CV	85
	Action words	89
	Contents	91
	CVs by date	92
	Skills-based CVs	101
	Keeping up to date	101
	Linking the covering letter and CV	102
	Summary	103
7.	**Application Forms**	**104**
	Preparation	104
	Contents	105
	Those difficult questions	109
	Final words	116
	Summary	117
8.	**Online Applications**	**118**
	Take care!	118

Practise		118
Email		120
Downloading		123
Keep a copy		123
Extra help		124
Summary		124
9.	**Convincing at Interview**	**125**
	What employers are looking for	125
	How interviews work	126
	Preparation	127
	Awkward questions	132
	More help	138
	Two-way process	139
	Over the telephone	140
	After an interview	142
	Summary	142
10.	**Should You Take the Job?**	**144**
	Over the moon	144
	Quite pleased	144
	Anxious	146
	Disappointed	146
	Keep getting rejected?	146
	Extra help	148
	Alternative lifestyles	148
	Summary	152
11.	**Glossary of Job-hunting Terms**	**153**
	Appendix – Working with a Computer	**157**
	Internet connection	157
	Internet service providers	157
	Searching the Web	158
	Setting up a Web-based email account	164
	Word-processing	166
	Saving onto a CD	170
	Printing a copy	171
	Index	**175**

Acknowledgements

We would like to thank the following organisations for allowing us to publish images from their websites:

www.gigablast.com
www.peoplemaps.co.uk
www.alec.co.uk

About the author

Jackie Sherman spent over 12 years as a careers adviser, working with undergraduates including many mature students at a number of British universities. She then ran her own business designing CVs before training as an IT and Adult Basic Skills tutor.

Since 1995 she has run numerous workshops for the unemployed or people returning to work after a career break, as well as training courses for administrative staff. She has spent time working for Age Concern providing drop-in sessions for older people and writes a regular 'You Can Do IT' column for the Over-50s website www.laterlife.com.

Her previous books include two aimed specifically at older people: *Getting the Most from your Computer* and *Everyday Computer Activities*, both published by Age Concern.

About this book

Many people approach job hunting in a piecemeal fashion, flicking through the first available newspaper or ringing up companies suggested by friends. However, if your search is approached in a logical manner, you can make sure that every angle is covered and that you are not missing out an important step in the process.

This book has been written to cover all aspects of finding work from thinking about your goal to what to do if no job materialises.

Finding work is hard, but it can be made easier if you use the wide range of facilities offered to you by computers. Throughout the book you will find suggestions and tips on how to do this for all your job search needs.

Please note: Websites come and go. Useful sources of information that were accessible when this book was written may now have disappeared. In the same way, new, exciting websites are sure to have appeared a few months after publication. So when reading this book, bear in mind that the websites listed are merely suggested places to visit: use your search skills to find more up-to-date advice, guidance and help for your job hunting.

(1)

Introduction

At some time in our lives, most of us need to apply for a job. At the age of 50 or more, many of you will still be hoping for full-time employment, but others may be looking for a satisfying part-time job: a way to earn extra money and have something interesting to do for a few hours a week. You may even be planning to take on a number of part-time or temporary posts (portfolio working) or look for an unpaid but rewarding voluntary placement. Whatever type of work activity you hope to take up, you will need to decide what direction to take, find the opening, make an application and succeed at interview.

Very few people enjoy the experience, but by taking it one step at a time and preparing well, stress can be avoided and you may soon be looking forward to your new position.

To be successful in any job search, you will need to answer the following questions:

1. Do you know what you want to do?
2. Can you find enough vacancies?
3. Is an advertised job right for you?
4. Can you present yourself on paper in the best light?
5. Will you come over well at interview?
6. Should you take the job if it is offered?

All these topics, and many more, will be fully covered in the book.

CHANGES TO THE CURRENT POSITION

If you are over 50, you already know how much you have to offer. However, you may not know that by 2010, 40 per cent of the workforce will be aged 45 or over, and the proportion of older people in the population is growing.

Carrying on working later in life is going to be far more common than it is now, and there are even changes that have been made to the state pension to encourage you to do so well into your 60s and 70s if you want to.

Age discrimination and the law

From 1 October 2006, it will become unlawful when employing or training people to discriminate directly or indirectly on the grounds of age. This means that employers cannot mention age in job advertisements, or use age as a reason for rejecting an applicant or limiting their promotion, unless there are exceptional circumstances that may well be tested in court. For example, some employers may feel they can justify fixing a maximum recruitment age based on particular training requirements or the need for a reasonable period of employment before retirement. Harassment on the grounds of age will also become unlawful.

Although in many ways the new law will be to the advantage of older people, it may also mean the end to positive discrimination schemes that some enlightened companies have been running.

Retirement

It is expected that the law will abolish mandatory retirement ages completely, so that an employer would always have to use performance as justification for dismissing someone. If a retirement age is retained, you can retire earlier than the age limit but cannot be forced out of work before then.

The new law will mean that anyone continuing to work into their 60s and 70s will be entitled to the same pay and benefits as younger colleagues, and the fact that experienced staff may be more expensive could not be used by employers to justify any reduction in benefit levels.

Pensions

According to the Department of Works and Pensions, the State Pension age will stay at 65, and no one can be forced to work beyond that. However, you will be free to work part time while drawing a pension so that working longer may be more attractive. There are plans to:

- provide a better deal for people who choose to draw their State Pension beyond their State Pension age

- allow people to continue working for the same employer while drawing their occupational pension

- raise the earliest age that a pension may be taken from age 50 to age 55.

State Pension deferral

You can put off claiming the State Pension when you reach State Pension age, or choose to stop claiming it after having claimed it for a period. If you choose to put off claiming it for a while, you are now able to get a higher State Pension or the choice of a one-off taxable lump sum payment when you do finally claim.

This change is designed to give you more choice in how and when you retire by making it more attractive to delay taking your State Pension.

COMPUTERS AND JOB SEARCH

People applied for jobs long before computers were invented, but they can help make your job search far easier.

Here are just a few of the ways you can use a computer to aid job-hunting:

- writing letters of application
- preparing a personal list of your skills and experiences – a CV
- learning about different types of work
- searching through job vacancies
- finding out more about an employer
- using email to send off for information or submit an application form
- applying for a job online.

An added bonus after using your computer for job search, if this is new to you, is that when you prepare your applications, you will feel more confident about including 'computer literacy' in your list of skills.

Computer access

One problem many people have is that they don't actually

own a computer. If you are in this situation, there are now a number of places that offer computing facilities – either free or for very little cost.

1. Public libraries are gradually installing computers – either in the main library area or a dedicated room – and at the time of writing you can book a free session whenever you want one.

2. Many colleges and education departments run courses attended by mature students. If you decide to take a class, you will have your own access code and can use the computers available in study areas and libraries.

3. Most high streets now boast one or more Internet or Cyber cafés. These are coffee shops where you can pay for computer use by the minute or hour and have a drink at the same time. If you worry about the costs, they are ideal for a quick search or to check your emails.

4. Job centres and careers services may provide free machines for their clients, to search for information or prepare a letter of application. They may also run special classes that include IT facilities which you can use to help in your job search.

To carry out all the tasks you might want to undertake, you won't need anything more than a basic computer system. However, it should offer the following facilities.

Printing
You will need a printer that will produce clean, crisp copy

and that will allow you, if necessary, to use your own choice of good-quality paper.

In public places such as libraries or colleges, this may be difficult as the printers may have been loaded with large amounts of standard copy paper and may be used continuously by a range of people in the same room or at networked computers throughout the establishment. This can make it very difficult for an individual to use their own paper. In such cases, it might be better to save your work onto removable storage media such as floppy discs or CDs and print important documents elsewhere.

Internet access

Whatever machine you have, it must have a reasonably up-to-date operating system such as Windows 98, 2000 or XP so that it can function properly when connected to the Internet. Ideally it will use a browser such as Internet Explorer or Netscape (programs that allow you to view web pages) offering all the normal functions including viewing pictures, printing pages and saving links to websites you may want to revisit.

(If you are not an experienced computer user, see the Appendix for full details of how to set up an Internet Service Provider account and search the World Wide Web.)

ORGANISING YOUR JOB SEARCH

Although you may hope that your first application is successful, being realistic is going to serve you far better in the long run. It is quite common to have to apply to a number of jobs before you are offered a position, and so it is a good idea to organise yourself. This prevents common errors such as forgetting to follow up an outstanding letter, missing an interview, losing the name or phone number of the person you need to contact, or writing to the same organisation twice without realising it.

Start a hand-written or word-processed document or even a spreadsheet and put in basic information about every job that interests you or for which you have applied, such as:

1. Job title
2. Contact details
3. Date you sent off for information
4. When you applied
5. Interview dates
6. Outcomes
7. Your comments after reflection or if you received feedback.

It is also a good idea to start a folder where you can keep copies of your application forms, letters and CVs as well as newspaper adverts, company brochures and job descriptions. They will then be easy to refer to before an interview or when completing a new form.

(2)

Knowing What You Could Do

You may be lucky enough to know exactly what type of work you want. Perhaps you have decided to continue using your professional qualifications or you enjoy working in a particular area and have decided to concentrate your job hunting here.

However, if you are dissatisfied with you present work and are looking for a change, or if you have had a history of unplanned jobs or are coming into the job market after a long gap, it can be extremely difficult to decide on the right direction to take or know which would be the best jobs to apply for.

If you have ever visited a careers specialist, you will have been asked to think about yourself, so that you could answer these questions:

- What are your strengths and weaknesses?
- What are you good at?
- What do you enjoy doing?
- What are your needs?

At the end of the session, you may have been given a printed list of jobs that would suit you best.

Sadly, it is not always easy to find the right type of work this way. Many jobs do not ask for a fixed set of skills or interests. In real life, very different people can be happy in the same job.

What happens is that each person will spend time on the parts that interest them most.

Take the job of: **office assistant at a doctor's surgery**.

Peter: likes people, so enjoys talking to patients. He spends as much time as possible at the front desk or on the phone, being helpful and friendly.

Catherine: is shy with people, but well organised. She spends most of the time sorting out patient records, checking prescriptions or sending samples to the lab. She also likes to keep the computer records up to date.

Bill: is interested in medicine. He spends time listening to the doctors and nurses talking about patients, tries to find out about illnesses and reads the notices and leaflets in the surgery.

As long as they carry out their tasks properly, all three assistants can be successful and happy in their work.

WHAT MAKES A GOOD JOB?

To find out what sort of job you might like, think about one you have had or wanted or that you know something about. List four good and four bad things about it.

Here someone has broken down two different jobs in this way:

Shop assistant

Good:	Bad:
Meet people Can buy cheap goods Working with ... (food, cosmetics, jewellery, etc.) Reasonable pay	Boring when the shop is not busy Work Saturdays Stand on your feet all day Have to handle money

Careworker in a day centre

Good:	Bad:
Help others People to talk to Not too difficult Part-time option	Poor pay Few young people around Long hours Unpleasant tasks, e.g. cleaning up

You will notice that these lists, and probably your own, are often more to do with **working conditions** than the job content, as these can be the real reason people enjoy or dislike their work.

WORKING CONDITIONS

Jobs offer many choices. Here are some to consider:

ASPECT	CHOICES
Working hours	9–5 Flexible or part time Shift work Work over a weekend
Place of work	Outside Office, hospital or school Work from home
People	Customers Mainly children or older people Many colleagues On your own

Training	On the job At a college None
Demands	Physical work A job where you live in Time often spent travelling
Pay	Highly paid Low pay Risky, e.g. commission-only
Travel	Long journeys Work locally Home based
Main tasks	On the telephone At a computer Using your hands Physical In public
Risk	Can be dangerous
Sector	Industry – service or manufacture Media Public service With animals or on the land
Perks	Discount when you buy in-store Cheap travel Sports club membership Medical insurance

SKILLS AND ABILITIES

Even if all the conditions are right, it is no good if you are unable to do the work. So you need to be very clear about what skills you can offer.

How to analyse yourself

To help you draw up a list, look at the different areas of your life where you would have used or learned a skill.

(Even if you are confident about what you can do, this exercise is helpful in adding skills that you might have overlooked, and identifying where you gained them, which will help when you apply for jobs and need to back up your statements.)

School or college
However far back in time it may have been, you will have gained skills when you:

◆ Studied for an exam or course, e.g
  – subject-related skills
  – practical skills
  – writing, note-taking, etc.
  – analysing
  – study skills, e.g. managing your time.

◆ Won prizes or awards, e.g.
  – sporting
  – passing exams
  – art or craft
  – clubs, societies, national schemes.

◆ Were a member of a successful team or group, e.g. young enterprise (set up a business)
  – debating
  – band
  – acting
  – sport.

◆ Carried out extra duties, e.g.
  – prefect
  – class representative
  – community work

   – taking visitors round

   – acting as mentor or on a helpline

   – DJ at social events.

Training courses

Whether through work or in your own time, you may have:

◆ Learnt a trade, e.g.
   – bricklaying
   – electrical repairs
   – shoe mending.

◆ Learnt a skill, e.g.
   – computing
   – driving
   – life-saving
   – taking pictures with a digital camera.

◆ Attended a short course, e.g.
   – first aid
   – telephone skills
   – public speaking
   – using a new piece of equipment
   – interviewing
   – wine tasting.

Personal skills

Ask your family or friends what they would say are your strong points. You might be good at a number of things, including:

◆ Organising, e.g.
   – parties

- meetings
- fund-raising
- builders working on your house.

◆ Helping others or cheering them up, e.g.
- looking after small children
- caring for an elderly relative
- visiting people who are ill
- listening when someone is grieving or depressed.

◆ Coming up with new ideas, e.g.
- planning surprises
- solving problems
- finding ways to save money
- running a business from home.

◆ Practical tasks, e.g.
- decorating
- gardening
- cooking
- mending things.

◆ Persuading people, e.g.
- raising money
- finding members or participants for a choir or club.

◆ Leading groups, e.g.
- taking charge on holidays or trips
- chairing a parent/teachers association
- setting up a club or society.

Leisure activities
Informal but extensive learning and the development of many skills takes place through clubs, societies, religious activities, hobbies and other leisure interests.

Have you been a member of a club or society involved in any of the following?

- Politics
- Religion
- Language and culture
- Wine or food
- Art or craft, e.g. photography
- Music
- Walking or sports
- War games or role play.

Have you any hobbies?

- Arts or crafts, e.g. painting or wood-carving
- Collecting things
- Running, yoga or keeping fit
- Singing
- Making models.

What do you do in your spare time?

- Clear land or waterways
- Go to the theatre or cinema
- Bowling or ice skating
- Surf the Internet
- Play an instrument
- Ride a horse
- Sewing
- Bird watching
- Visiting ancient monuments.

You will also have gained a variety of skills from books, radio and television programmes or self-study material.

Home

Whether or not you have some form of employment, you still carry out day-to-day tasks at home that develop skills which could form the basis for a new job. Some of these might include:

- cooking
- gardening
- decorating
- shopping
- managing money
- clothes-making
- mending the car
- raising money for a favourite charity
- looking after a parent or small children
- answering the phone
- cleaning
- planning holidays
- paying bills
- helping with homework
- collecting or delivering people
- organising, e.g. music lessons, repairs, deliveries, etc.

Work

There are three main areas where you may have gained skills:

1. In any past or present job.
2. Working as a volunteer.

3. Spending time on work experience, job shadowing or helping a work colleague, friend or family member with some of their work-related tasks.

For example, you may have developed one or more of these skills:

◆ Job-specific skills, e.g.
  – hair colouring and cutting
  – shoe mending
  – plumbing
  – baking
  – dry cleaning
  – breeding animals.

◆ General, transferable skills common to many types of work, e.g.
  – handling money
  – filing
  – organising collections of items
  – answering the phone
  – dealing with complaints
  – listening
  – driving a delivery van
  – producing reports
  – making bookings
  – entering items into a database
  – reading timetables
  – cataloguing
  – cleaning.

Achievements
You don't need to have run a multi-million pound empire

or gained a saleswoman of the year award to have successes you can draw on that will help build up a picture of yourself and identify new skills or capabilities.

Think about any job you have had, as well as your leisure, personal and academic activities and in each case pick out something you are proud of. For example, you might have:

- made friends with a colleague who was originally antagonistic

- worked out how to use a complex piece of machinery

- persuaded a publisher to take your first short story

- learned to swim despite a long-term fear of water

- negotiated a higher salary

- gone on holiday on your own for the first time

- helped a friend through bereavement

- planned a particularly successful course, seminar or conference.

For any such activity, you will have used personal or practical skills that might otherwise be left off your skills list. In many cases, these achievements could be added to a CV or application form as evidence of your personal qualities or abilities.

Skills categories

Some people find it easier to identify their skills by grouping them under different categories. For example:

1. Dealing with people – perhaps you are good at advising, listening, interviewing, persuading, selecting or organising.

2. Dealing with things – these might include inspecting, mending, constructing, sorting, preparing or designing.

3. Dealing with ideas – would you say you were successful at adapting, evaluating, questioning, planning or presenting?

4. Being artistic or creative – can you write, draw, sing or work with colours?

Skills analysis questionnaires

If you find the task of analysing yourself hard, there are hundreds of books available providing self-assessment questionnaires and also a number of websites, often American but still valuable as a tool, that offer self-assessment online or material you can download for free.

One exercise is The Skills Park produced by The University of East London at www.uel.ac.uk. After completing the questionnaire, you build up a skills profile and are given advice on the various ways to use it.

Another online self-assessment test can be found at the American Careers InfoNet site which is part of the US Department of Labor's Career OneStop suite of products: www.acinet.org/acinet/skills_home.asp. This site encourages you to complete a very full interactive questionnaire on the range of skills you believe you have.

Finally, the University of Minnesota has produced a useful site on transferable skills at www.d.umn.edu/student/loon/car/self/career_transfer_survey.html. Although aimed at students, it is helpful to anyone who is not sure what they can offer an employer. The questions are divided into five broad areas including communication and human relations. After rating each skill from 0–3 you can click the 'Sum it all up' button at the end of the list to display your overall score.

Skills you do not have

As well as making the most of your talents, try to avoid things you find hard, if these are going to be a major part of the work. Although it is tempting to accept such a job if it is offered and hope you can muddle through, it could turn out to be your worst nightmare if you simply cannot cope with the day-to-day tasks.

To help you decide what these may be, look back over your life and think about:

- Any academic subjects you failed. Were you always poor at subjects involving numbers, computers, foreign languages, writing or remembering information? Or were you clumsy with your hands, e.g. in art, craft and design technology or cookery?

- Job-related tasks that were too difficult. Did you find it hard to talk on the phone, stand up to people, display goods, speak at meetings, take messages or write your reports?

- Hobbies you could not master. Have you given up painting and drawing, music, model-making or carpentry? Were you poor at yoga or sports? Did you forget your lines in the theatre group?

- Personal traits your family would say are your weak points. Are you clumsy and break things? Disorganised and lose things? Poor at saving your money? Or are you shy and find it hard to talk to new people?

IMPROVING YOURSELF

If you want to use a skill but you are not good enough or you don't have the experience that is needed – don't give up. There are many ways you can make yourself more attractive to an employer. Here are four to consider:

- Gain the skills on a course or by teaching yourself.

- Work as an unpaid helper: e.g. as a classroom helper before you apply for jobs as a Learning Support Assistant in a school.

- Take a lower-level job to find out more about a new area of work and show you are motivated. If, for example, you take on a job made available by someone going on maternity leave for three or six months, you can still add the skills and experience you gain to your application.

- Work part time. Even if you want a full-time job, starting as a short-term, temporary or part-time worker often leads to full-time employment later. For example, it is common for people joining a 'temping' agency to be offered a job as a permanent member of staff in one of the offices or factories where they work.

Courses

Colleges and community classes all have a sprinkling of people well into their 70s, so it is never too late to learn a new skill. Many adult classes are part time, but if you decide to take a full-time training course, there may be grants to help you if it leads to a recognised qualification.

Local libraries will have prospectuses for your local College of Further Education or University Continuing Education Department as well as day and evening classes run by Community Education Centres.

One of the most useful organisations developed over the last few years has been Learn Direct, which has a free phone number: 0800 100 900 and a website at www.learndirect.co.uk. Here you can search by region or subject to find courses available to you. These may be studied in the normal way in a classroom, taken online or delivered through a distance learning college.

You could also visit www.hotcourses.com for an alternative courses website. Although it appears to be aimed at people with degrees and even postgraduate qualifications, there is also an excellent selection of part-time and lower-level training courses to search through.

Finally, if you want to study on a residential course, a good place to look is the City & Guilds website at www.timetolearn.org.uk where you can search the database for weekend or one-week courses within easy reach or in beautiful parts of the country you might like to visit. As well as offering an attractive setting in which to learn, these courses are also an excellent alternative to a normal holiday as you will meet a range of people with similar interests and will be offered social as well as educational events in which to take part.

University of the Third Age (U3A)

Most towns have a more informal grouping for people no longer working which is part of the University of the Third Age (U3A). As well as offering a way to meet people, the members run different clubs and societies where you can learn new skills. Visit the central website at www.u3a.org.uk or call in at your library to find out the name of your local U3A secretary.

Study online

An alternative to a course taken in the community is to get started straight away and study over the Internet. U3A have started offering free, online courses so you may find a suitable topic from the list on their website. The BBC also offers courses ranging from languages to history, business and science that you can study if you visit them at www.bbc.co.uk/learning. Click the link to Adult Learning. Each page offers actual courses or relevant information as well as links to external sources of course information.

DISABILITIES

The law is very much on your side when it comes to finding employment if you have a disability. If this is a fairly new situation or you were not aware of the help that is available, visit your local Jobcentre Plus and speak to the Disability Adviser or check out the government's website at www.direct.gov.uk. This provides information on resources, training, finance and your employment rights.

INTEREST AND MOTIVATION

We all have likes and dislikes, and there are often skills that we do not want to use. It is important to take this into account when looking at jobs. For example: are you expert at drawing, but would hate to be an artist? Are you good with children, but would not want to work in a nursery or school? Or are you a computer whiz, but would never choose to enter data all day?

To find out what motivates you, look back over your life areas once more, but this time think about how keen you were, or how much you would like to carry out those tasks now.

Academic subjects
What were your favourite subjects and why?

Training courses
Which courses did you enjoy, or were there any that you would have liked to attend?

Personal skills
Are there some that you want to use in your work; or do you love animals, music, books, foreign places, etc, and would like to work in a related field?

Leisure activities
Do you have any hobbies or leisure interests you want to follow up as a career?

Work experience
Was there a job you really enjoyed, or work activities you want to carry out now?

Home
Is there an everyday activity that you would like to develop?

Values

Motivation is also very much tied up with our values. For example, do you see work as simply a way to earn money or is it more important to be recognised or to have a job where you can be independent? You may prefer to find work that allows you to be in charge, or you may decide you need a job that is a constant challenge or that gives you a real purpose in life. Some jobs are more likely to give you these things than others.

You may also need to take into account the ethos of the organisation, and how it treats its staff.

One final aspect of job choice is the type of employer you want to work for. Consider whether the *product* (e.g. tobacco, alcohol, computer games, chemicals or cosmetics) or *service* (e.g. working in a casino or betting shop, debt collection or money lending) is acceptable to you.

TYPES OF WORK

In many cases, careers decisions are made by looking at the range of jobs available and whittling them down to a manageable number based on your abilities and interests.

The choice of job can come from any direction, so you need to be flexible and open to opportunities. For example:

♦ Could you develop one of your hobbies?

♦ From your voluntary work, could you make contacts or become a manager of volunteers?

♦ If you currently have a job, would you like to work for a similar organisation or in the same field but for a different type of employer?

♦ Taking a non-vocational course such as yoga, flower arranging or photography could lead to becoming a teacher yourself – or why not write teaching materials or magazine articles about the subject?

♦ Listening to friends or family members talking about their jobs might inspire you.

♦ If you have experience that makes you an expert or especially sympathetic to people in difficult situations, you might be able to train as a counsellor or community worker.

♦ With practical skills in activities such as gardening, decorating or renovating property, there are more and more openings for such expertise.

♦ Are you driven to pottery, painting or making jewellery? This might turn into a job on the fringes of 'real' craftspeople if you are not talented enough to make a career as a professional, e.g. could you work in a gallery or craft shop or become a demonstrator of equipment?

◆ Have you seen a job you like on TV?

If you are looking for inspiration and like the idea of an interactive website, you could visit The Career Key, a free website set up by Lawrence K. Jones from North Carolina University at www.careerkey.org which offers an analysis of your skills, interests and abilities and links them to possible job areas.

You could also browse through some job profiles at sites such as www.connexions.gov.uk and www.learndirect-advice.co.uk.

Age limits

Although this book will emphasise the need to concentrate on finding the job that best suits your needs, you *may* want to enter a career or join an organisation that has an official upper age limit for entry which will not be affected by the forthcoming age discrimination legislation. To find if this is likely to apply to an area of work you have in mind, look carefully at the entry requirements within any job profile.

Salaries

Even if you find an attractive and suitable area of work, you need to know roughly the level of salary you could command. This is especially true if you need a minimum to support yourself or your family, if you are hoping to move into an unknown type of work or to a different part of the country, or if you fear you may be asked a question about expected salaries in an interview and don't want to end up accepting too low an offer.

Apart from checking the salaries displayed in job advertisements, you could try a web-based salary checker: one of the simplest can be found at www.paywizard.org.

WEBSITES FOR OLDER PEOPLE

It can be helpful to know what is out there for older people and which types of job or employer have helped them make a success of their job search. The Internet provides a wealth of useful information.

Many magazine-style sites have been set up aimed at older people that include articles, success stories and useful advice and links related to work. One of the more popular is Laterlife at www.laterlife.com.

The government is also looking into ageism and has established the website Age Positive at www.agepositive. gov.uk. It includes case studies, policy documents, facts and figures, details of companies that have a positive recruitment record and links to organisations trying to help older people get work. It is well worth a visit on a regular basis.

For general advice and links to various sources of information including pension details, the government has also set up an Over 50s website at www.over50.gov.uk.

CAREERS ADVICE

If you find self-assessment hard and need further information or want to talk to someone face to face about your choice, you may need to find a careers adviser or at least a good careers library.

All schools, colleges and universities have a careers office and offer help to their own students. They may also have information rooms open to the public.

Universities also publish a website, Prospects, at www.prospects.ac.uk that offers careers information and for mature students, the chance to email an adviser if you graduated during the past five years.

The government careers service, known in many areas as Connexions, is aimed at teenagers aged 13–19 and offers a range of jobs suitable for such young people including apprenticeship schemes. However, there is also help for older job seekers as advisers work with adults within what were formerly known as Information, Advice and Guidance partnerships (IAGP) but are now more often called Next Step partnerships.

Most regions offer guidance under the IAG or Next Step umbrella, including finding work when you are over 50. Phone the free national telephone number: 0800 1954 700 or go to www.nextstep.org.uk for a local phone number and information about what they can offer.

WHICH JOB TO CHOOSE

You should now have an idea of the working conditions that would suit you, the skills you can offer, the tasks to avoid, your main areas of interest and an overview of possible job types. Do they clearly point to one type of job?

For most of us, knowing ourselves better will not always be enough to lead to a narrow range of jobs that are just right. And if you are interested in a very popular area of work or one that normally has few vacancies, you will need to be flexible and consider alternatives.

A large number of people take a job because:

- they spot the advert
- the work is local or easy to get to
- they have enough of the right skills
- it looks interesting
- the working conditions are acceptable
- they manage to pass the interview.

The job may turn out to be ideal; a sensible starting point; good enough until something better turns up; or a big mistake.

To avoid making a mistake, think about yourself and test this against the job details for any job you are considering. Carry an **honest** picture of yourself at all times, so that you don't waste your time, but only apply for jobs meeting your needs and where your skills, experiences and personal qualities match those that are required.

SUMMARY

1. Different types of people can all carry out the same work as they will choose to spend more time on the parts they enjoy.

2. Key aspects of a job relate to the working conditions such as hours, location or pay.

3. Find out what you are good at by looking carefully at all areas of your life.

4. It is important to find jobs that motivate you so that you would enjoy the activities.

5. There are many ways to improve yourself if you do not have the abilities or experience that are required.

③

Finding Vacancies

Knowing what you want to do is no use if there are no jobs to apply for. So you must look in all the right places if you want to have a choice and find enough jobs to consider.

HOW YOU HEAR OF A JOB
There are six main ways you might find a job:

1. **An advertised vacancy**:
     - in a newspaper or magazine
     - shop windows
     - on a local radio station
     - at a jobs fair
     - the World Wide Web.

2. **Internally advertised at work**:
     - word of mouth
     - on a notice board
     - newsletters or bulletins
     - intranet (internal computer network).

3. **Through agencies**:
     - private recruitment agencies
     - job centres
     - careers services.

4. **Making a speculative approach**:
   – writing a letter
   – calling in for a chat.

5. **By word of mouth**:
   – hearing by accident from friends or family
   – asking people to look out for you at their place of work.

6. **Networking**:
   – This means making a positive effort to use business, social, family or other links to contact people who may know about new employment areas or organisations seeking recruits.

THE ROLE OF THE INTERNET

Over the last few years, the Internet has completely changed the way we live and manage our lives, and that includes job search. You will now find that, as well as special vacancy websites, most of the old methods for advertising jobs are also repeated on the World Wide Web. This includes websites set up by newspapers, employment (recruitment) agencies, job centres, employers and professional bodies.

To use your computer in this way, you must know how to search the World Wide Web. You will either have to use the correct web page address (known as the Uniform Resource Locator or URL) or visit the site of a search engine holding a database of thousands of pages that you can search using key words. Turn to the Appendix if you need advice on searching.

Email alerts

If you have an email address at home, college or at work, you may be able to set up an email alert system. Enter details of the type of job you want into forms on vacancy or newspaper websites and each week they will send you details of any jobs that match your needs.

Post your CV

Some websites allow you to publish or 'post' your CV so that employers can look at it. (Don't expect too much from this, however, as it is likely to be even less successful than advertising yourself in a local newspaper.) As long as the document is on your computer, floppy disk or a CD, clicking the Upload or Browse button will display all the files on your machine. Select the CV file and it will be sent direct to the site.

Note: Take care with this process as you can never be certain who will see your details. Check sites are password-protected and don't put too much personal information into a CV that you are posting online. You should find that good sites such as www.jobsearch.co.uk have details of their privacy policy, so read this before posting.

LOCAL NEWSPAPERS

These newspapers, sometimes delivered free, make most of their money from advertising cars, houses, services, second-hand goods and local jobs. Usually, the jobs are lower-level and will require fewer qualifications than those in national papers. This is because the employers will not be offering very high salaries and so will want to attract people who do not need to move house to take up the posts.

Examples of local newspapers that publish jobs include:

The Evening Argus (Brighton)
The Evening Echo (Essex)
The Oxford Times
Bristol Evening Post
South Wales Evening Post
Bolton Evening News.

If you don't mind where you find work, or you want to move to a job in a particular area, check out websites such as the British media online website at www.wrx.zen.co.uk/ britnews.htm. It has links to a wide range of regional newspapers and you can find which ones to order if you want to check the jobs regularly over a period of time.

NATIONAL PRESS

Not all nationally advertised jobs will be aimed at 'high flyers' and some should be available in your local area.

Daily newspapers such as *The Guardian*, the *Independent*, the *Daily Telegraph* or *The Times* have large classified sections full of jobs, and they offer different types of work on certain days. For example, if you want jobs in the **health or social services** sector, look at *The Times* on Tuesdays or *The Guardian* on Wednesdays.

If you want **secretarial** work, look at *The Times* on Wednesdays or *The Guardian* on Mondays or Saturdays.

There are special educational papers such as *The Times Educational Supplement* (out each Friday), but you will find **education** jobs in *The Guardian* and *The Times* on Tuesdays and the *Independent* on Thursdays. **General** jobs are usually advertised in the *Daily Telegraph, Independent* and *The Times* on Thursdays, or *The Guardian* on Mondays and Saturdays.

Online newspapers

Nowadays, all major newspapers have websites that offer a job search. If you carry out a general search, it won't matter which day you choose as all the vacancies published during the last few weeks will be on offer.

To find any newspaper website, type www.[newspaper name].co.uk into the Address box of your browser. Use the on-screen index to open the jobs page. There will normally be a quick search box and the chance to browse through all the jobs on the site.

You will also be offered a range of criteria such as job title, industry, region and salary from which to select an option. Complete these before searching if you want to narrow down the eventual list you will be offered.

MAGAZINES AND JOURNALS

Most hobbies are linked to a magazine and every trade and profession has its own journal, so it makes sense that they offer their readers job advertisements as well as articles and news.

There are far too many to list here, but call in to your local library or job centre, ask your newsagent or look on the Internet to find out which trade journal you should read if you want a particular type of job. You may have to pay for a few issues, but it could be the only way to find that special position.

Here are just a few examples, where the names of the journals show the type of jobs they advertise:

Campaign (advertising)	*Community Care*
Computer Weekly	*Nursing Times*
Building Estates Gazette	*Travel Trades Gazette*
Music Teacher	*The Grocer*
Electronics Weekly	*The Bookseller*
New Scientist	*British Journal of Photography*
Caterer and Hotelkeeper	*The Stage*
Housing Today	*Design Week*

Most, such as *The Stage* at www.thestage.co.uk, have an online version that you can visit to carry out an immediate job search. Some areas of work related to academic subjects also have an Institute such as the Institute of Physics (www.iop.org) and these will advertise relevant vacancies. Although mainly aimed at graduates or those with professional qualifications, there may also be support service posts advertised such as in administration or technical services, and there will be information on careers and advice on job-hunting in that subject.

Job categories are also represented. For example, if considering work in the financial sector, institutes including accountancy, actuaries, banking and tax have produced a joint careers and jobs website at www.insidecareers.co.uk.

Interim management
If you have been in a middle or senior management position and are looking for temporary work, perhaps to supplement a pension, interim management might be ideal as they can use your expertise to tide them over a difficult time, for one-off projects or when staff are ill. Companies will offer short contracts, usually between 3 and 12 months in length, and often the work can lead to longer-term involvement.

The main organisation offering advice and information on this type of work is the Interim Management Association and information about it can be found on the Web at www.interimmanagement.uk.com.

SHOP WINDOWS
Many things are advertised in shop windows, including goods and services for sale and rooms to let. You can also find local part-time jobs in this way such as cleaning, childminding, bar work, seasonal fruit-picking, catering, delivering or packing.

As well as your local newsagent, look at notice boards in supermarkets, church halls, playgroups, village halls, leisure centres or rural post offices.

Always check out the employer very carefully – it is likely to be a local garage, pub or shop or even one person working from home, and you will have less protection than with a larger employer.

HOME WORKING
Take particular care if you are offered work from home

such as making things or stuffing envelopes and they ask for a deposit for equipment or a registration fee. This can indicate that you might never be paid for your work as it will be continually rejected as sub-standard. Visit the website www.homeworking.com for advice on avoiding scams when working from home. You may also find that the promised new jobs website for anyone keen to find work from home is now up and running.

CALLING IN PERSON

Shops, offices, restaurants and factories may advertise their own vacancies on boards or in windows. If you are confident enough, call in and try to have a brief chat with someone about possible vacancies, or at least leave your CV.

AGENCIES

These are contacted by employers who tell them about jobs that the public do not see. Instead, the agency will find people on their books who they think might be suitable, and those names are put forward to the employer directly.

High-street agencies can be found in most towns. They may offer general jobs of all types, or cover a certain type of work such as secretarial, industrial, technical, manual work, publishing or nursing. The jobs are commonly temporary or short-term but if you are any good, an employer may ask you to stay on.

If you want the type of work they provide, here are the steps to take:

- *Register with the agency.* Provide all your personal details and work background and explain what you are looking for. They usually ask for a CV or will help you write one. In some cases, you may have to take a test, e.g. to check typing skills, and nowadays you will have to take in proof of identity such as your passport or driving licence.

- *Keep in touch.* They may contact you if a job turns up, but check with them on a regular basis to make sure they keep you in mind.

- *Look on their website.* Increasingly, they will expect you to check here and contact them if you see a job you like.

- *Go to a few interviews.* They should arrange some for you and, even if you are not sure you want the job, go along for practice. Always check to find out what feedback the employer gave the agency if you do not get a job offer.

Do not pay any money. Agencies will be paid by the employer, and should never ask you for money to register.

Reed, Manpower, Office Angels, Select Appointments, Blue Arrow and Driver Hire are some of the many agencies that have offices across the UK.

VACANCY WEBSITES

If you put the words 'vacancies UK' or '[type of job] + recruitment' into any search engine box, you will be offered a wide range of websites. When visiting any of the sites, you may see 'featured' jobs that they are selling harder, but it is best to choose the job **type** and **region** and then click the search button or press Enter on your keyboard.

If the search offers one or more jobs of interest to you, there will be a link to further details, an online form or an email address which you can use to send off for more information.

Note: However good the search, you will find the one drawback of job-hunting in this way is that you cannot treat it like a newspaper and skim the page of adverts by eye to spot a job you might not otherwise have thought of.

With the Web, you are forced to select specific criteria so that only a limited number of jobs will be presented to you. One way round this is simply to type in a location or very general job title and browse through all the jobs on offer.

General websites
These will let you search for any type of job. There are hundreds, but you could try:

www.fish4jobs.co.uk
www.totaljobs.com
www.ukjobs.com
www.monster.co.uk
www.alljobsuk.com.

Specialist websites
Other sites mainly advertise jobs from a single sector. These sites come and go all the time but a few examples include:

Museums (www.museumjobs.com)

Public sector (www.jobsgopublic.com or www.lgjobs.com)

Construction (www.constructor.co.uk)

Computing (www.vnu.co.uk/jobs)

Academic or scientific institutions (www.jobs.ac.uk)

Nursing and health (www.nursingnetuk.com or www.jobsinhealth.co.uk)

Newspapers (www.holdthefrontpage.co.uk)

Retail (www.retailchoice.com).

When it comes to community work, one website www.charitypeople.co.uk offers links to not for profit organisations that want staff – permanent, temporary or as volunteers.

The sites all work in similar ways to the general job sites, offering regional maps or boxes so that you can search locally or by job type.

Older job seekers

A number of websites now offer vacancy information aimed specifically at older job seekers. However, as they are relatively new in the field, don't rely on them alone to provide enough suitable vacancies. Here are a few you could try:

www.maturityworks.co.uk focuses exclusively on the needs and interests of workers over 35.

www.jobsfortheover50s.co.uk not only features vacancy information but also statistics on employers' attitudes to applications from older people.

www.fiftyon.co.uk offers careers advice as well as access to jobs for anyone over 50.

The website Friends Reunited that puts former school or college students and work mates together has now set up a, jobs website at www.friendsreunitedjobs.co.uk.

Finally, if you want to work in London, you could make use of www.wiseowls.co.uk catering for anyone aged 45–65.

COMPANIES ONLINE

Somewhere on most company websites – often at the bottom of the page – you will find links to information on the company itself rather than its products or services. One link may be clearly labelled, e.g. 'Join our staff', 'Job opportunities', etc.

International Sites: United States |

Join Associates | Join our staff |

On other sites, it may be hidden behind a general heading such as 'About us' or 'Customer Services'. At Debenhams, for example, if you click the Customer Services link, there is a 'job opportunities' link at the bottom of the screen. This will open the vacancy page and you should now be able to see what jobs they have, as well as find new links to application forms or email contacts when sending your CV.

Finding the websites

If you don't know the exact web address (URL) of an employer, most UK companies have the address www.[name].**co.uk** but international companies end in **.com**.

URLs for employers that are not businesses end differently:

Educational establishments end **.ac.uk**, e.g. Exeter University advertises academic and support staff jobs at www.exeter.ac.uk.

Government, both national and local, ends **.gov.uk**, e.g. Devon County Council regularly needs staff and will advertise vacancies at www.devon.gov.uk.

Charities and societies end **.org.uk**, e.g. Oxfam when it requires workers will place notices on its website at www.oxfam.org.uk.

JOB CENTRES

If you are unemployed and receiving benefits, you may be familiar with the system and will know that the name has changed to 'Jobcentre Plus'. If you are a new job seeker, call in to look through the vacancies and get help with your training or job search needs.

You may find free copies of useful newspapers or trade journals and if you have been out of work for 6 months you should be offered advice from a Personal Adviser and free courses to help you with your CVs, letters or preparing for interview.

You can join a special programme, New Deal 50 plus, if you are aged 50 or over and have been receiving benefits for at least 6 months. If you prefer to read about what is involved before approaching a job centre, full details can be found at www.newdeal.gov.uk.

JobCentre Plus also offers its jobs online, so you can carry out a search at www.worktrain.gov.uk.

SPECULATIVE APPROACHES

Many jobs are never advertised. An employer may decide that he or she needs an extra person in the workplace and will then contact somebody they know is looking for this type of work.

As well as work with established organisations, jobs often arise when a factory, supermarket, hotel or sports centre opens in a new area or a company decides to expand. Be the first to spot the possible vacancies by looking at your local newspaper or listening to local radio on a regular basis.

To be contacted, you first need to get in touch with the employer and make sure your details are 'on file'. Phone first if you can to discuss possibilities, or simply write speculatively.

(See Chapter 5 for advice on how to write the letter.)

NETWORKING

Some people view this as a far more effective way to find employment than waiting to spot advertised vacancies. Networking involves building up a network of contacts through a direct approach – usually in person or by phone but you may need to send an initial letter or email.

The key to a successful approach is to ask people for information or advice rather than actual jobs. In some cases, it can be easier if you can arrange an informal chat over a drink or coffee, but in all cases you must avoid being seen as 'pushy'.

Starting with people you know well such as family, friends, past employers, ex-colleagues, tutors, your doctor, hairdresser or chiropodist, tell them your background, the sort of work you are interested in as well as your special skills or experience and ask if they know about any likely job openings. They may be aware of expansion plans in their own companies, or of promotions, takeovers, internal restructuring or other developments that might provide you with a suitable opportunity.

If the people you first contact cannot help, ask them to suggest someone else and follow these people up systematically. If possible, ask if you can quote the name of the original contact, e.g. 'John Davies suggested I contact you…'.

There are also networks already in existence that you can tap into such as alumni or business organisations so you must be prepared to go to a few meetings or lunches to make new contacts.

When you approach someone you have never met it may be something that you feel uncomfortable about. To make it easier, start by finding out something about them. Express an interest in their work before telling them about yourself.

In all cases, make sure they have your contact details. Although they may not have anything to offer at the time you first make contact, something may develop and you need to be sure that they are in a position to tell you about it.

Eventually, you may make contact with someone such as a head-hunter or recruiter who will actually have a job to offer and you may find you are in the happy position of having an interview for a job that has never been advertised or even having a job created specially for you.

ADVERTISING YOURSELF

As well as posting your CV on employment websites as described earlier, you could put your own advert in the local newspaper – they often have an Appointments Wanted section. It can be quicker than writing to every possible employer in the area, and your advert may be spotted by someone with a job to offer who has not yet advertised it in the normal way.

Keep the advert very simple and include:

- ◆ the type of job you want
- ◆ your main skills, qualifications and experience
- ◆ one or two key personal qualities
- ◆ contact details.

> Cook, 16 years' experience in city centre hotels with City & Guilds Food Preparation and Cooking NVQ Level 1, looking for pub or restaurant work. Cheerful and hardworking. Please contact ...

SUMMARY

1. There are many different ways that you can hear about jobs, not just through advertised vacancies.

2. Check the local papers, national press and specialist magazines on a regular basis.

3. If following up a card in a shop window, take care if you are offered home working and are asked to pay a fee.

4. Register with an agency to find out about jobs that are never advertised.

5. Use the Internet to find more vacancies on agencies' or employers' own websites. Some have been set up to offer work specifically to older job seekers.

6. Phone or write to employers you would like to work for, even if you do not know they have any jobs available.

7. Make use of any contacts to build up a network of people you can approach about possible jobs.

8. Advertise yourself in case an employer spots your details.

4

Is the Job Right for You?

Employers do not want to waste time. When they have a job vacancy they will try to word the advertisement carefully, to give readers as much information as they need. In this way, it will be easy for anyone thinking of applying to select themselves out – if the job is not right for them – or in, if they think they can do it.

ANALYSE THE ADVERT

When you see an advertisement in the newspaper, or receive job details by post, it is a good idea to underline every mention of skills, experience, interests or working conditions so that you are very clear what is on offer.

Example

Customer Services Assistant

Campsforkids is a young and dynamic business, providing fun-packed, safe and stimulating children's activity camps.
We require an assistant for our Customer Services Manager. You will need to:

- Be an enthusiastic and energetic team player
- Have excellent verbal and written communication skills
- Be able to take, process and administer bookings and deal with all aspects of incoming enquiries
- Be motivated, conscientious and flexible in accommodating the needs of a seasonal business

We offer a salary circa £16,000 dependent on experience plus 25 days holiday. If you would like to contribute to our success, please apply in writing by 19 March to:

Requirements

Most jobs can be divided into four main areas, although these can overlap:

◆ skills, abilities or experience
◆ interests
◆ personal qualities
◆ working conditions.

There is also the 'hidden agenda' to consider, where you must guess what might have been left out of the advert.

In the example:

Skills, abilities or experience
They will expect you to offer some of these:

◆ Worked with children or parents
◆ Have experience of children's activities
◆ Have experience of children's camps
◆ Know about a Customer Services department
◆ Can work in a team
◆ Have been someone's assistant
◆ Can deal with administrative tasks
◆ Have taken bookings
◆ Good verbal skills
◆ Good written skills
◆ Can deal with enquiries, e.g. phone, email, fax, letter.

Interests
To look forward to this job day after day, you need to:

◆ Enjoy the idea of providing services for children

- Want to be involved with a company running activity camps
- Enjoy taking bookings
- Would like an administrative job
- Want to use verbal skills
- Want to use writing skills
- Want to work in a team
- Want to work for a dynamic business
- Would be happy working with younger members of staff.

Personal qualities

You need to feel that you are:

- Enthusiastic
- Able to fit into a young, dynamic business
- Flexible, e.g. about tasks or hours
- A team player
- Energetic
- Conscientious, i.e. an accurate, careful worker.

Working conditions

Do the following suit you?

- An office-based job
- Much use of phone or computer
- Salary £16,000
- May be very busy at some times of year
- 25 days' holiday
- Mainly young people in the office/company.

You also need to check out:

- Journey to work each day
- The hours.

Hidden agenda
- Could you deal with angry parents who might phone to complain?

- Would they expect you to work overtime when they are very busy?

- Is training offered, or will you have to learn on your own?

- Is training compulsory, in case you do not want to study any more?

- Will you have to travel around the camps as part of the job?

FINDING OUT MORE

The job in the example above provides some helpful information in the advertisement, but it would be useful to know even more before you made your decision.

You should always try to find out background on the organisation and possible competitors, the type of work and any extra information that is relevant.

Can the employer help?

Some employers suggest you write in for further information or a job description, or phone for a chat. **Always** follow this up.

Job descriptions usually show details of hours, salary, who you report to, the main duties of the job, its purpose and the 'person specification'. This lists the personal qualities they hope you will have, and the qualifications, relevant experience, skills and specialist knowledge required. It may even be graded and say whether the qualities are essential or just desirable.

If the job advertisement is short, a job description is the only way you can be sure you will address *all* the key points when you provide evidence to show you are right for the job.

Further sources
If no further details are provided, you will need to look elsewhere. Here are some possible sources of information:

1. Most medium to large-sized organisations will now have their own website. Visit this to find out more about them, such as their products, services, structure and general feel. (There may even be information on the actual job you are hoping to do.) Send off for brochures or the annual report if these are offered.

2. Companies are legally obliged to publish information about themselves. If you go to www.carol.co.uk, for example, you will be able to carry out a search for a particular company report.

3. Colleges, schools and universities all have careers libraries that hold information on employers and types of work, and there is usually a careers or Connexions office in every town.

4. If you have a friend or family member who is in similar work, ask them to tell you more about it.

5. For jobs that are around everywhere, e.g. sales assistant, travel agent, bus driver, classroom assistant, local government officer, dental nurse, etc. – call in to a local shop, depot, school, office or dental practice. Pick up any leaflets about products or services and ask if a member of staff has time to talk to you about their work.

6. Your local library will have a reference section holding some careers leaflets or books.

7. Websites: as well as the company's own website, search for information on the work in general. View job profiles (as described earlier).

8. If you know of a similar company or employer, phone for *their* brochure or information as it may be helpful.

9. Read job adverts carefully. Even if the actual jobs are not right for you, the descriptions will provide lots of information on different types of work.

Tricky facts

There are things it can be very hard to find out, yet they can make a difference to how you feel about the job and whether you want it or not.

These may include:

♦ where you will buy lunch or spend your lunch-hour
♦ if car parking is provided
♦ if there are any perks
♦ any overtime requirements.

Use your 'private research' if you can to find the answers.

Note: If you have not found answers before an interview, do not dwell on these aspects of the job here or you will look as if you are not interested in the work, only the extras. Ask about them just before you finally accept a job offer.

DECISION TIME

Having analysed any job you are thinking of applying for in as much detail as you can, you will be able to:

- check out each point carefully
- decide if there are more positive than negative aspects
- know if the job *feels* right.

No person can have every skill or experience that is asked for. If you have the key ones and would be interested in doing the work, then it is time to apply.

SUMMARY

1. Analyse a job advert carefully to make sure you are clear about everything that is needed.

2. Think about what is not mentioned — the hidden agenda.

3. Find out as much as you can about the employer and type of work.

4. Only when you know exactly what is involved can you decide whether it is right for you to apply.

5

Applying in Writing

To put all the right things into your application, you need to know what employers will want to see. If you have never employed anyone before, it can be easier to do this if you first imagine you are an employer yourself.

WHAT EMPLOYERS LOOK FOR

Imagine that you run a small newsagent and you are looking for a sales assistant. What would you look for in a job applicant?

Here are a few ideas:

Skills and abilities
Can handle money
Can add up accurately
Fit enough to stack shelves and move heavy items
Can speak politely to customers,
Able to use the computer and till.

Motivation
Interested in working in a shop
Happy to get up early or work late
Enjoys talking to customers
Willing to be flexible
Keen to learn.

Personal qualities
Gets on with people
Pleasant to have in the shop
Honest and reliable.

For this job, a successful applicant will show that they have all the relevant skills and interests and will try to indicate that they have the personal qualities that are needed.

They will also want to show that they have taken care with their application so that it is neat, clear and has no spelling or grammar errors.

EMPTY STATEMENTS

It is no use stating that you have the skills that are needed without backing your statement up with facts. Don't say you are 'good with people' or 'have an excellent telephone manner' unless you can show it is true, and offer evidence in some form that, if necessary, could be checked.

You will not be asked to take in certificates or badges, but it must be clear that you have carried out an activity that would give you the required skill.

In your application, provide evidence by showing that you gained or used the skill through:

- attending a class
- passing an exam
- gaining a certificate, award or cup
- working in a job where you used the skill
- used it in other areas of your life, e.g. as a volunteer,

parent or home owner or connected to a hobby or other leisure activity.

You will also need to show that you have the interests or are motivated. Again, provide evidence by showing that you have chosen similar types of activity or working conditions before or have good reasons to want that type of work.

Example

TECHNICIAN TO ART, DESIGN AND TECHNOLOGY DEPARTMENT, WILKINSHAW COMPREHENSIVE SCHOOL

We are seeking an adaptable, lively and enthusiastic person to support the work of this diverse and busy department. Much of the work will be directed towards the practical areas and therefore some skills within this broad context would be an advantage. An interest in education and the ability to work as part of a team are also highly desired.

15 hours per week, term time only. Pay: £13,071–£13,701 pro rata.

Please send letters of application together with a CV ...

Carrying out our analysis, we can see that the job is asking for:

Skills, abilities or experience
♦ Worked in a school or with children
♦ Practical – able to work with tools, equipment and materials, ideally in the art and design field
♦ Have been a technician

◆ Can cope with a busy place
◆ Have worked in a team.

Interests
◆ Education
◆ Working in a school
◆ Dealing with children 11–18
◆ Art, design or technology
◆ Teamwork
◆ Busy department
◆ Technician tasks – setting up, tidying away, making or repairing models, etc.

Personal qualities
◆ Adaptable
◆ Lively
◆ Enthusiastic
◆ Supportive
◆ Team member
◆ Can cope when busy.

Working conditions
◆ In a school
◆ Most of the time in workshops
◆ Part-time
◆ Term-time only
◆ Not a high wage
◆ Busy department.

PROVIDING THE EVIDENCE

The ideal job to apply for is one where you have carried out the actual tasks before, but in many cases this is not going to be possible. In our example, what evidence could you put down to show you can do the work and would be the right person for the job? For every point that is in the advert or that you think they will look for, ask the question: **Have I ever ...?**

Skills or experience

Worked in a school – e.g. acted as parent helper or volunteer, been on a school committee, given a talk or helped with special events.

Worked with children – e.g. been a childminder or looked after relatives or your own children, helped out at a playschool, nursery or a children's club or taught any skills to children at a class or Sunday School.

Developed practical or technical skills – e.g. carried out any work using tools such as craftwork, car or bike maintenance, mended household items, used a computer, had photographic or art hobbies or built or mended models.

Been a technician – e.g. chemical, animal, materials, food, photographic or engineering.

Been part of a team – e.g. played a team sport or been a pub quiz team member, worked closely with others, been in a planning group or met to make joint decisions, run something with another person.

Shown an interest in

Education – e.g. in your interests, reading, past jobs, etc.

Children – e.g. at home, in your hobbies, jobs or reading.

Art, design or technology – e.g. in your hobbies, jobs, academic subjects or home activities.

Other factors
Worked in a busy place – e.g. as a paid worker or volunteer, especially during the Christmas or holiday period.

Had to support others – e.g. at home, in your leisure time, at school or college, perhaps as a mentor, counsellor, hospital visitor, trainer of new staff or simply as a colleague or friend.

Had to be adaptable – e.g. by doing extra tasks at work, changing hours or patterns of work when asked, juggling several different part-time jobs or leisure interests at the same time, or moved house often.

Had a reason to want term-time work only – e.g. needing to look after children in the holidays.

For any question where the answer is **Yes** – make sure you add the details to your application.

FOLLOW THE INSTRUCTIONS
Always check these very carefully and do exactly what is asked. For example:

◆ Have they asked for any extra documents to be included?

◆ Do they want referees now?

♦ Do they want more than one copy of your CV or form?

♦ Have they asked for a covering letter *in your own handwriting?*

♦ Is there a particular address to send applications to?

One exception is where you are asked a question you do not want to answer. This may include:

♦ reasons for leaving your present job
♦ your employer's contact details for a reference
♦ your current salary.

You have three choices: ignore the question completely, say details will be provided later, or put the answer at the very end of your letter or CV so they have to read your full application first.

(Advice on how to answer difficult questions on forms is offered in Chapter 7.)

When to include a CV

If you have spent hours typing a CV, you will want to use it for all your job applications.

Do send it when the advert says:

♦ Apply in writing
♦ Send a letter and CV
♦ CVs are accepted
♦ Write to us at ...

Do not send it when you are told:

◆ To complete the application form (if your CV would add no new information)

◆ CVs are not accepted.

WORD-PROCESSING

To create documents that will be attractive to potential employers, nowadays you must be able to use a word-processor. The advantages of producing everything on a computer include:

◆ being confident that your work is easy to read and looks professional

◆ the ability to customise your basic details for a range of different job applications

◆ using the delete and retype facilities and spelling and grammar checkers to correct errors

◆ sending the same, individualised letter to a number of different employers

◆ updating your details without retyping all your documents

◆ saving copies of everything you send out for future reference.

(Later in the book, you will find advice on setting out letters and CVs, but for any documents that you want to create, you will need to know the basics of word-processing. These are set out in the Appendix.)

SENDING OFF FOR DETAILS

When you apply for a job, you are competing with many other people. If you do not know as much about the job as they do, or do not apply correctly, your application will not be as strong and may even be rejected. (This is not part of the application process, and only needs a very simple letter or message.)

Write, phone or email if the advert says there is:

further information
a job description
an application form.

Important: Make a note of the closing date for the job application. If you don't receive the information or application form within a week, phone or write again to make sure it is not lost in the post. It then won't be too late to apply if they send you another copy.

Writing a letter

If there is no named person to write to, start your letter: *Dear Sir or Madam* or *To the Personnel Officer* and end: *Yours faithfully.*

Include:

- your full contact address
- today's date
- the job title and any reference number
- where you saw the advertisement
- what you want
- who they send it to.

On a computer, the convention is to set out everything down the left-hand side of the page and to leave out extra commas.

---

13 Severance Close
Worthing
Sussex
BN2 4YY

2/2/0X

Dear Mrs Eaton

Receptionist (Ref. RP4)

Please would you send me an application form and further information about the job recently advertised in The Worthing Gazette.

Yours sincerely

Joanne Jacobs (Mrs)

Using email

Email is now indispensable – whether you want to respond quickly to job vacancies or send off your details cheaply to a large number of potential employers.

Some machines have email systems such as Outlook Express, First Class or Eudora installed on them. They allow you to read and write messages without having to connect to the Internet.

If you are using public computers, you can set up a web-based email system and use it for all your job search needs. Turn to the Appendix for full details on how to register for your own email account.

To ask for job details by email, open your email system and click New Message. Complete the following boxes:

To: the full email address of the recruiter
Subject: job title and any reference number
Main window: The reason you are writing and your postal address, in case information cannot be sent electronically.

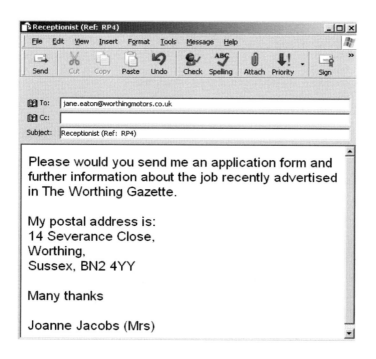

COVERING LETTERS

Every time you apply for a job, you should include a covering letter. This is the **most important** document you will supply to an employer. It will be read first, before any other documents. It must be short and easy to read – in good English with no spelling or other mistakes.

It should show clearly that you:

- know what the work will involve
- can do the tasks
- are interested in the job
- have addressed any key points made in the advert.

It helps if you can also show you:

- will fit in with other people at work

- have a positive attitude to what is offered, e.g. extra training or future jobs in the company (if these are available)

- will not be too ambitious or expect too much from a low-level job.

Appearance
- Unlined, white or off-white, good quality A4 paper.
- Sent in a large envelope so it will have no fold lines.

General advice
Keep a copy of all your letters, so that:

- if you have an interview, it will remind you what you said

◆ you can check on the date it was sent, if there is a long delay before you hear from them

◆ you will know who you have applied to, in case you need to contact them

◆ if you are unlucky and your application is not successful you can look back at what you wrote to see how it could be improved

◆ having prepared a letter once, it is quick to send off copies to other employers.

Plain English
At all times, keep your letter simple: don't use three words where one will do.

Not: *I was of the opinion that...*
But: **I thought**

Not: *At this particular point in time I am...*
But: **I am now...** (or **I am currently...**)

Not: *pertaining to*
But: **about**

Sent with a CV
Some employers accept a letter without a CV, but this is not common. Include your CV unless you are told not to. (Details of how to create a CV can be found in the next chapter.)

Layout
1. *Contact details:* Your full address, to include a contact telephone number and/or email. Place it at the top

and in the centre or on the left of the page. Do not include any phone numbers, e.g. for work or in a shared house if you do not want to be contacted there.

2. *Who you are writing to:* The name, job title and address of the recruiter. Use **Ms** if you do not know if a woman is married or not. If there is no name in the advert and you cannot find out who to write to, word the details in a general way, e.g. To: Head of Personnel or Human Resources.

3. *Date:* Today's date.

4. *Greeting:* Formal greeting: i.e. Dear Mr... or Ms... or Dear Sir or Madam.

5. *Vacancy:* The full job title and, if included, a reference number, placed on its own line and emphasised, e.g. bold, underlined or in capital letters.

6. *Reason for writing:* The first paragraph should explain why you are writing – to apply for the job – and where you saw the advert. Some employers advertise jobs in several different papers and online at the same time, so it helps them know which advert was successful in attracting applicants.

7. *What you can offer:* You must provide a *summary* of the **relevant** skills, experience, interests and/or personal qualities that you can offer which you have identified by analysing the advertisement. They will show that you know what the work will involve. Even though the details are covered in your CV, you **must** include them here. *Remember* – if the letter is not good enough, no one will bother to read your CV.

24 Larkin Place
Headington, Oxford
OX2 3ZT
01865 5578990
m.tompsett@btinternet.co.uk

Ms Rose Welcombe
Training Officer
Stenton Services
Ridley Road
Swindon
SW2 4FF

3/9/0X

Dear Ms Welcombe

ASSISTANT PROPERTY MANAGER

I would like to be considered for the above post advertised in The Daily
Echo.

For the last two years, I have been helping my brother look after two flats
that he owns in Oxford. I have carried out basic repairs and decorated
several rooms.

After attending a computing course at Oxford College, I was asked to
work in the office where I have been keeping landlord details up to date
and sending out reminders to tenants who were late paying rent.

I have really enjoyed the work and would now like to join a larger
company and make use of my experience in property management.

I enclose my CV and look forward to hearing from you.

Yours sincerely

To make your letter easier to read, put your points into two or three short paragraphs rather than one long one.

8. *Motivation:* Include a paragraph to show you are interested in this type of work, or the employer, and motivated to stay and develop your career.

9. *Ending:* End the letter by saying that your CV is enclosed. If you used the recruiter's proper name, end with **Yours sincerely**. If not, end **Yours faithfully**.

10. If you have any problems about interview dates, e.g. a forthcoming hospital visit or holiday, a likely change of phone number or were asked for anything specific such as owning a car, include them here.

11. *Last things:* Check the letter for spelling or grammar mistakes and do not forget to enclose your CV in the envelope.

Sent with an application form

If you are applying for the same job as before, but they asked you to fill in a form, your letter will be very similar. If the form was designed properly, you should have put most of your relevant skills and experience down already so you may find you can keep the main section slightly shorter.

End the letter by saying your form is enclosed and check for spelling or grammar mistakes. Do not forget to enclose the application form in the envelope.

24 Larkin Place
Headington, Oxford
OX2 3ZT
01865 5578990
m.tompsett@btinternet.co.uk

Ms Rose Welcombe
Training Officer
Stenton Services
Ridley Road
Swindon
SW2 4FF

3/9/0X

Dear Ms Welcombe

ASSISTANT PROPERTY MANAGER

I would like to be considered for the above post advertised in The Daily Echo.

As you will see from my application, I have spent two years helping my brother look after his two flats where I gained experience in maintaining the properties as well as office procedures.

I have really enjoyed the work and would now like to join a larger company and make use of my experience in property management.

I enclose my completed application form and look forward to hearing from you.

Yours sincerely

REFERENCES

Before you start applying for jobs, find two or three people who will be happy to speak up for you and say you are honest, reliable, hard-working and carried out your work or other responsibilities well. These are your *referees* and the documents they provide (or details over the phone) are known as references.

Who to choose

One will be expected to be your current or most recent employer, a supervisor if you have been a volunteer, or a tutor if you have attended a course of study. For a second reference, it is now less common to ask for 'personal' references (to say you are of good character) than another employer or tutor.

If it is hard to find the second or third referee, choose a person you know in the community, e.g. vicar, scout master, solicitor, doctor, local head teacher or bank manager, or who you know through your leisure interests. It helps if they have 'status', e.g. as shown by their job title or address.

Referees should not be relatives.

Always pick someone yourself and check with them that they are happy to do this for you. It is a good idea to send them details of the job, so that they can write a relevant reference.

Change your referees if different people are more relevant to a certain range of jobs. For example, the Chair of Governors or Head Teacher of the school where you are a parent governor would be ideal for jobs related to education, community or committee work. But your evening class IT teacher might be better for jobs related to computing or general office work. Do not give an unnamed member of staff, e.g. *Head of Personnel* or *Training Officer*, as they may not know you personally or be able to make positive comments.

Note: there is no rule that says you must use your immediate superior for a reference. If you do/did not happen to get on well with them, try to find someone else in the organisation who could comment favourably on your work.

On the CV?

Unless the job advert states that referees must be included with your application, you can choose to leave them until later and provide the names and contact details separately. If you will *always* use the same people and they are happy to be contacted at any time, add them to your CV. If they may change, include them at the end of each new covering letter.

What to include

You will need to put down as many of these as you can:

◆ Full name including title (e.g. Dr, Mrs)

◆ Position such as *Fitness Instructor* (mention if this is a past job, e.g. if they have left or are now retired)

◆ Postal address

◆ Contact telephone number

◆ Email address

◆ How you know them e.g. if they are a current or previous employer, teacher or work colleague, etc.

For example:

Dr Ian Bramley
Lecturer in Electronics
Weston College of Engineering
Ridgeway Lane, Cheshunt
CB1 3RT
Tel: 01756 4452778
(Tutor for Robotics evening class)

Disclosure

If you don't want people at work to know you are looking for another job, make it clear on the CV or form that you do NOT want your current employer contacted unless you are offered an interview or the job.

As mistakes can happen, you could even put:

Current employer – details to be provided.

SPECULATIVE LETTERS

These letters are very similar to covering letters sent with a CV. The only difference is that there is no advertised job to apply for. Instead, you are writing to ask if they have any jobs and, if not, will they keep your details on file so that they will be able to get in touch if a job arises.

Who to write to

If you want your letter to be taken seriously, try to reach the right person. Unlike an advertised post, there will be no named contact and so you must find out the best person to apply to. Phone up the main switchboard, call in e.g. to the reception area, or send an email to the general address asking for this information.

♦ In organisations with a separate personnel department, ask for the name of the Head of Personnel or Human Resources.

♦ For specialist posts, find out the name of the head of that area, e.g. *Head of Information Services* or *Centre Manager*.

♦ With small organisations, e.g. a garage, pub, school or shop, find out the name of the owner, landlord, head teacher or manager.

If you *cannot* find a name, address the letter to 'Head of Personnel' or 'Centre Manager' rather than just 'The ... Company'.

Subject

As with covering letters, your letter should have a subject to show what it is about. Use a general heading:

E.g. Job Opportunities

Or *Future Vacancies*

Opening sentences

Instead of a first sentence that says:

I would like to apply for the post of ...

You need to have a reason for writing that you can put in

the letter. Here are some examples:

- The work is in a sector where you have experience or an interest.
- They have jobs that you are trained to carry out.
- You have a connection with this employer.

For example, you could word your opening sentence as follows:

I have three years' experience helping to look after two rented flats and wonder if you have any vacancies in property management within your company.

Or

I have spent six months working as a volunteer with Property Management Inc. in Australia and I am now hoping to find a permanent job in the UK where I can make use of this experience.

Contents

This is similar to covering letters sent with a CV – tell them the skills, experience, qualifications, interests etc. that you can offer.

Most important: give them full contact details. If you think these might change over the next few months, you should include an alternative phone number or address.

Have a job in mind

Although you may not always be applying for a specific post, this will help you make the most of your relevant background. For example, you could apply to a pub for a job as bar staff, cleaner, cook or accountant; make sure you decide on the position and then describe your relevant background skills and experience.

Send a CV
They will need the information ready when they do contact you.

Last sentence
Instead of '*I look forward to hearing from you...*' you can write:

'I look forward to hearing from you *should any suitable vacancies arise.*'

Follow up
If you send in a letter but don't hear anything after a week or two, phone the employer and check that they have received it.

◆ If they know nothing about it, say you will send another copy.

◆ If they say they don't want to employ you – thank them for considering you and ask them to keep your details in case a job comes up in the future.

◆ If they show an interest in you, be prepared for an instant interview on the phone. Before you contact them, plan out answers to a few obvious questions they may ask. (See advice on telephone interviews in Chapter 9.)

Example of a speculative letter:

14 Grundy Avenue
Maidenhead, Berkshire
RH4 5TY
01232 5638887

Head of the Research Laboratories
Pharmacol Ltd.
Cheshire Lane
Maidenhead
RH8 2ER

14 May 200X

Dear Sir or Madam

Job Opportunities

For the past six months I have been working as an assistant in the Urology Department of Maidenhead Hospital and wonder if you have any vacancies for laboratory technicians within your company.

After leaving school with 5 GCSEs including biology and maths, I spent a number of years managing a newsagency before deciding I wanted a change of career. Two years ago I joined the MRI Unit at the hospital and spent a year organising patient records, dealing with appointments and writing up notes.

Since moving to the Urology Department, I have learned how to take samples and enter results into the main database. Part of the work has involved monitoring patients who have been trialling the Pharmacol drug Epex and so I know something of how it works.

I have really enjoyed working in the laboratory and making more use of my biology, and would find it very rewarding to work for a pharmacology company making drugs such as Epex that improve patients' lives.

I enclose my CV and look forward to hearing from you should any suitable vacancies arise.

Yours faithfully

Peter Douglas

SUMMARY

1. If you imagine you are an employer, it can help understand what they might be looking for.

2. Always back up statements about yourself with evidence in terms of actual examples of where you gained the skill or experience.

3. Follow the instructions on how to apply and make sure you send the right documents.

4. Send off for details with a simple letter or email.

5. Prepare a covering letter carefully, to emphasise why you are the right person for the job.

6. When supplying referees, choose people who will support your application.

7. Write to an employer to show interest in working for them even if they have no vacancies at the present time. Your details will be kept on file and you may be contacted if a job becomes available.

(6)

Producing a CV

A CV (curriculum vitae) is a document in which you present personal information about yourself including your contact details, past or present work experience and academic record. In some places, it is known by the American term 'résumé'.

If given a choice between applying using an application form or a CV, most people prefer the CV. This is because *you* choose what to include and how to present it. With a form, the layout and content are set by the employer.

WHAT IT IS NOT

A CV should not be used on its own when you apply for work as it cannot address the details of any advertised vacancy. That is the job of a **covering letter.** In each letter, you will choose which parts of your background to emphasise.

The CV should be used to provide factual information about your past and to back up your statements about the skills, abilities and experience that you can offer.

Although a CV *can* be rewritten every time you apply for a different job, this should not be necessary. Most people only need one CV, but if you are applying for quite different types of work, you could produce two versions to suit the different groups of jobs. For example: if you wanted a job in TV *or* a general office:

CV1 – would stress your leisure interests of film-making and theatre and a voluntary job in hospital radio

CV2 – would include more detail of your office jobs, voluntary work for a housing association and your computing skills.

APPEARANCE

- ◆ Word-process and choose a type large enough to be read easily.

- ◆ Use a single side of A4 for each page – staple pages together if you produce more than 1 page.

- ◆ Send it in a large envelope so you do not have to fold the paper.

- ◆ Check that there are no spelling or other mistakes.

- ◆ Make the layout easy and quick to scan, with space round each section.

- ◆ Give sections clear headings.

- ◆ Make use of bullet points and bold or underline for emphasis, but do not use too many different types of font (letter styles) which can make documents look fussy and hard to read.

- ◆ Do not include photos unless asked to do so.

- ◆ Use good quality, white or off-white paper.

DESKTOP PUBLISHING

Although most people word-process their CVs, software is now available to help you design a professional CV quickly. One package is Microsoft's Publisher, but you can also buy CDs with CV-writing programs on them.

If using Publisher, open the program from your **Start** menu and you will be offered a catalogue of ready-designed publications. Select *Resume* and the style you prefer.

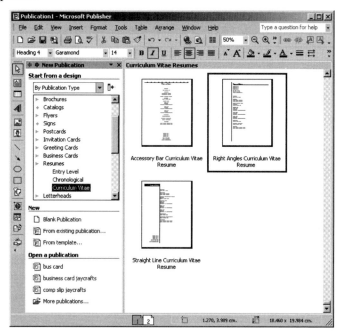

When it opens, you can make various changes to the layout and colour but must then amend the content of each section and the order in which information is presented.

Just click in any box to edit the contents in the same way that you would word-process a document.

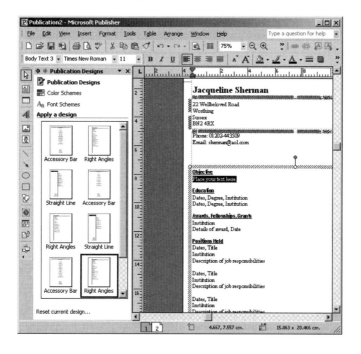

Use your mouse to drag boxes to different positions when the pointer over the edge of a box shows a van.

TYPES OF CV

There are two main ways you can present your background information in a CV – by date and by skill.

By date (chronological)

Each section can either start with the current position and work backwards, or start with the earliest example and work towards the present day. It will depend on whether the most recent example is the best place to start.

For example, if you are applying for jobs where your school or college subjects are more relevant than later courses, set out your *academic record* starting with your secondary education.

If your recent job is most relevant, set out the *work experience* section starting with the work you do today.

By skill
This type of CV is also referred to as 'functional'. Pick out examples of different skills, achievements or experience that you want the employer to know about, and then add details of how and where they were gained.

As you may have used the same skill or had similar success across a number of jobs or hobbies, the actual dates are less relevant in this type of CV.

Which layout to choose?
Some jobs, e.g. in sales, marketing, public relations or the media, seem more suited to a skills-based CV as employers will be looking for achievements and successes.

If you have had a career break or a patchy record of work, or you feel your age will be a definite disadvantage, it may also be better to use a skills-based CV. Gaps will be harder to spot and there is less emphasis on actual dates: put details of education and work as bullet points with no years.

Length
The CVs that are easiest to read are two pages long. Much longer, and they will include too much detail or go back

too far into the past. Shorter, and they will not include enough information to 'sell' you to an employer.

A great error made by many job applicants is to tell it all. This is not what is wanted. Use every means to summarise, shorten or omit detail that is really not relevant or that won't show you at your best.

Summaries

If you have had a very long career but feel you need to include all the details, try to summarise your earlier experience so that it fits into a short paragraph. To make your summary of more interest, you could drop in one or two named examples.

For example: *1970–1978: Working for a number of different hotels and restaurants, including the Savoy Grill in London, involved in food preparation with an emphasis on hygiene and safe handling and storage.*

If you have studied many courses, cut back or cut out the less relevant school or early college record to leave room for important details, or group similar education or training together.

Not:
  1993 Introduction to interviewing
  1994 Telephone skills, including dealing with complaints
  1994 Advanced interviewing
  1995 Writing reports, etc.

But: *Since 1992, a variety of in-house training courses covering interviewing, listening, report-writing and handling telephone complaints.*

Too short?

If you have little to say, or are new to job-hunting, try to add more details to the sections you include so that your CV fills at least one side of A4 paper. For example, instead of:

> *Voluntary work: Helping in a local primary school*

you could say:

> **Voluntary work**: *Since 2003, spend one morning a week at a local primary school, working with small groups of children in Yr 5 and teaching some music sessions. Help organise Christmas concerts of recorder music and carols.*

Page numbers

For a CV that is longer than one page, always add page numbers and your name to each sheet.

What you can leave out

When you write a CV, there are no rules and you can choose what to put in and what to leave out. There is no need to put your age/date of birth, health record, married status, leisure activities or ethnic background in a CV unless they will offer an advantage.

For example:

◆ Working with the elderly, with mature customers, or for many of the jobs where experience really matters – your age can be a positive factor.

- Working with non-English speakers – your own ethnic background will be helpful.

- In education – the fact that you have children can be useful.

- For careers work – a mixed background of different jobs is an asset.

- Leisure activities will be crucial in performing arts, crafts, museums or other hard-to-get jobs.

- Working with the disabled – having overcome a disability will be seen as an advantage. (Also, many companies have policies that encourage disabled people to apply.)

A question of age

If you want to play down your age but do not want to design a skills-based CV, take care with school dates or years in work as people can work out a rough birthday very easily.

If you would not be missing out very important details, leave out the school years altogether, move the education section to the end and only provide information on the more recent periods of work.

ACTION WORDS

A CV can be a mixture of full sentences, phrases and bullet points, so use whatever English is needed to make the meaning clear and easy to read.

When you describe any activity, instead of the name of the activity or job or 'working as...' followed by the job title, describe what you did.

Not: *Working as an Assistant Florist*

But: *Assistant Florist* – checking supplies, designing wreaths, planting bulbs and taking orders.

Not: *Football*

But: *Play football for the Gas Board and involved in training a local under-13s team.*

Use **Action** words. Examples include *organising, preparing, solving, training, changing, answering, planning, assisting, advising, selecting*, etc.

♦ Research Assistant – *analysing cell samples, writing lab reports and training junior staff.*

♦ Clerical Officer – *answering the telephone, making appointments, filing and photocopying.*

♦ Receptionist – *taking room bookings, answering queries from guests and checking bills.*

Avoid starting too many sections with 'I'.

Not: Boxtree Hotel, Windermere
I worked as a receptionist on the hotel desk

But: Boxtree Hotel, Windermere
Receptionist – taking room bookings, answering queries from guests, serving in the restaurant and checking bills.

CONTENTS

Time

Unless it is very important to show the exact length of time, keep to **years** and not **months** as this allows you to 'lose' gaps or short-term jobs. Putting exact months encourages employers to work out how much time is missing.

Humour

We all have a different sense of humour. It is a good idea to keep your application 'light', but not try to be funny unless you are applying for the job of a comedian.

How to start

For some strange reason, many people head their CVs: 'CURRICULUM VITAE'. Instead, put your name and brief contact details only.

PETER HARGREAVES
22 Westmorland Road
Oxford, OX12 4XP
01865 3373982
p.hargreaves@scotts.co.uk

As there may be hundreds of applicants for any job, do not clutter up the top of your CV with personal details – the recruiter may not read further than half-way down the page. If necessary, add more personal details in a section at the end.

Now start the detailed section with the appropriate subheading for your major selling point. For the one area that presents you in the best light or is the most relevant – work, education or leisure – put it first.

If you are weak in one area, e.g. you have a poor academic record, put this section at the end – keep it very short, or leave it out altogether!

But take care: when you read a job advertisement, you look for the 'hidden agenda'. Remember that an employer will do the same with gaps in your CV.

Contact information

Always include the name you wish to be known by (i.e. a nickname if you do not use your full name), full postal address, telephone number(s) if daytime differs from evening, and your email address. If you spend time at different addresses or can only be contacted at certain times, add this information somewhere. Remember – this is how they will contact you, so it must be correct and up to date.

Sections

There are four or five main sections that most employers will expect to see, and they can be in any order, but your name should always be easy to find at the top of the first page.

CVS BY DATE

1. Education and training

There are no rules that say you must include all details. The more qualified you are, the less important your early school or college record will be, and some courses will be quite unnecessary. Use common sense to decide whether to include details or not. For most people, here are the details normally included:

♦ Unless your academic record is so poor you are going to ignore it, note down secondary schools, colleges and external training courses attended, with names and dates. If you are highly educated, you may prefer to start with A-levels or your degree.

♦ Include courses taken, awards with grades (if good) or just single (or grouped) subjects if poor, e.g. *5 GCSEs including maths and English.*

♦ As you get older, only go back in time as far as is relevant to the type of work you want to do.

♦ Leave out any failures in subjects that are not relevant to the work.

♦ If you failed any courses but gained useful skills, include them but do not pretend you passed an exam. (Remember, you may leave an awkward gap if you do not mention a period of one or more years when you were studying.)

Not:

1998–1999   <u>Diploma in Administration</u>
            Did not complete 2-year course

But:

1998–1999   <u>Diploma in Administration</u>
            First year of course, studying comput-
            ing, marketing and business.

- If relevant, add more detail to show exactly what you learnt.

- Is there anything extra you did that you are proud of? Make sure you add it to your CV. For example,
  – community work
  – raising money
  – winning prizes
  – being a club official
  – Duke of Edinburgh award.

- If you are on a relevant or interesting course of study or have enrolled for one starting later in the year, always include this on the CV, leaving the finish date blank or adding 'Present' or 'Now'.

Starts Jan 200X St. Michael's College, Dartford
Two year diploma in garden design.

2. Work experience

All jobs including paid and unpaid, long- or short-term can be included. You will usually include the years, name and location of employer (but only town and/or county – not full postal address), job title and main duties you carried out.

For any activity, it is most important to say what you did and what responsibility you had, and to use action words as described earlier.

Grouping

For similar types of work, or if you have forgotten the dates, group them together to make them easier to read. If it is not clear from the job title and duties, you could also mention what you gained. For example, if you had a range of temporary jobs, you could word this section as follows:

1991–94   *A range of temporary clerical jobs working for solicitors, insurance offices and banks. Gained experience of office procedures and how to keep information secure.*

Achievements

However low-level your jobs may have been, looking back over your working life you can probably identify things that you achieved or were proud of, or a particular success story. Can you include these in the job details?

2002–2004 **Cotswold Training Company**
              Administrator – organising training schedules, booking student places, handling payments and acting as the first point of contact for all tutors. *Several of my suggestions for new courses were introduced successfully into the programme.*

Overcoming problems with work experience

If you have little or none:

◆ Take on some voluntary work **now**.

◆ Rename the section, e.g. *Work Skills,* or do not include it at all.

◆ Create a skills-based CV so that details of actual employment are replaced by what you can offer.

If it is not relevant, e.g. you are changing career:

◆ Take on some unpaid work in the new work area to show motivation and gain experience.

◆ Explain clearly in your covering letter why you are changing.

◆ Pick out the transferable skills you can offer so that you won't be labelled by your past experience. Whatever you did, you can still show that you were a success, managed staff or gained promotion, etc., or that you have a number of useful skills to offer a new employer.

If you are 'over-qualified':

◆ Emphasise why you are interested in the job (to show you would not be bored or want to move on too soon).

◆ If your reasons are shallow, e.g. for an easy life, concentrate on explaining what you can offer.

If you were bringing up a family:

For anyone currently in this position, it is a very good idea to take on some voluntary work or course of study so that you can include it on your CV. Home study is ideal for this e.g. taking an Internet or distance learning course or buying a self-help book.

For a previous period of time, there are two different ways to treat this section:

◆ For a CV by date, mention this period briefly in your Work Experience section if there would otherwise be a large gap, and add any skills or experiences you gained during the time here or in other relevant sections.

◆ Instead of '*Bringing up a family*', put down any work-related activities you undertook during this time.

For example:

> 1992–2000   *Self-employed: designing and selling greetings cards*

3. Leisure interests

Most people either leave this section out altogether or put down two or three main hobbies or group a number of related activities together. Only include interests if they meet one or more of the following criteria:

◆ Relevant to the work you are seeking.

◆ Likely to show you in a good light, e.g.
  – gained a high level of skill
  – achieved success
  – started something new
  – could lead people
  – worked in a team
  – needed to be brave, reliable or flexible, etc.

◆ Helpful in balancing a one-sided CV, e.g. if you have worked alone in all your jobs, include a leisure activity that shows you get on with others.

◆ Unusual subjects to catch their attention and that will be interesting to talk about during an interview.

Do not include a list of hobbies for no good reason, and never say you watch TV and go to the pub unless you want to work in TV or the drinks industry.

Group similar activities under headings:

Not: Singing in a church choir
Playing the electric guitar
Knitting
Taking photographs
Writing songs for a band

But:
Music   Singing in a church choir
Playing the guitar and writing songs
Crafts   Knitting
Photography

4. Skills

This is the place to add skills and abilities that you want to include but that do not relate to a particular time, employer, hobby or course of study. Examples: driving, foreign languages, first aid, computing or many of the tasks carried out when bringing up a family. Indicate the level you reached or how you gained the skill. For example:

French – Spent several summers working in Paris so can hold a conversation and read the newspapers.

Decorating – Completely re-decorated several rooms in our house, including stencilling and applying different paint effects.

Computing – Taught myself word-processing and using email.

5. Other

Your own background may suggest a new section that should be included in your CV. For example, have you lived abroad? Have you run your own business? Have you been involved in major charity work or a special event or worked as a volunteer for a long period or for an unusual organisation? Or are you a member of any professional bodies or have produced any publications? Either head it *Other* or add a suitable heading and set out the details in the same way as all the other sections.

6. Personal statement

Some people like to add an extra item often referred to as a *profile* at the start of their CV – a short statement or summary of their background or the type of job they are looking for. If you want to include this section, keep it short, factual and general, unless you are happy to re-type your CV for each application.

Note: If you use an employment agency, they may send out your CV without a covering letter. In this case, a statement on the CV can provide the reasons why you should be considered.

Example: *Landscape gardener with 15 years' experience running apprenticeship schemes seeking a position as a trainer within local government or the private sector.*

Example of chronological CV:

Daisy Martin
24 Long Lane
Dymchurch, Kent
DM4 3BX
01204 5562341

Work Experience:

1986–88	Heston Library, Bristol *Assistant (part-time)* – reorganising the video and CD collections and designing posters to advertise events
1991–95	Hamilton Business Centre, Dymchurch, Kent *P.A. to Centre Manager* – making appointments, organising conferences and meetings and booking space at the Centre
1996–Present	Active Theatre, Dymchurch *Volunteer* – helping with costumes, advertising and collecting props for all the productions

Academic Record

1966–71	Settington Comprehensive School, Colesworthy
GCE:	7 including maths, English and art Studies textiles for 2 years
Marshall Prize	Art in the Community – awarded for best poster to improve the environment
1988–90	Mottrill College of FE, Bristol OCR. New CLAIT – computing course covering word-processing, spreadsheets, databases, presentations and desktop publishing

Leisure Activities

Crafts:	Started a club for lace-makers locally and now have 25 members. We recently completed an altar cloth for the local church with each member adding a panel.
Community work:	Member of the local BBONT and spend week-ends clearing up common land. We are making a pond for local children to use as a nature study area.

SKILLS-BASED CVS

Look at the details of several jobs you want to apply for and pick out some key skills they all mention and that you can offer. Place these at the top of your CV with evidence to back up your statements. You can then continue with general summaries of your work experience, academic record and leisure activities.

Key Skills

Communications
- Telephone and email contact with business clients
- Persuading local shop-keepers to provide free items for a theatre group

Computing
- OCR New CLAIT certificate in Word, Excel, Publisher, Access and PowerPoint
- Producing posters using image editor Paint Shop Pro

Teamwork
- Working with other helpers in environmental work
- Organising a team to create a work of art together

Initiative
- Setting up new craft club that is so successful it is now over-subscribed
- Reorganising a video library to attract new borrowers

KEEPING UP TO DATE

If you have already produced a CV, don't forget to amend it on a regular basis. Check it every few months or make changes immediately if you have:

◆ been on a training course

- had a different job
- changed your overall career plan
- taken up a new hobby
- moved house or changed email address
- been involved in an interesting project or event.

At the time, you may think you won't forget such details, but it is very easy to leave out one of these pieces of information if you have to rush to create or amend a long CV at a later date.

Have confidence that all your details are correct and up to date so that you can take advantage of a job advert spotted at the last minute.

LINKING THE COVERING LETTER AND CV

Once your CV is ready, you can be selective and use any aspect of the information to support your covering letter. Put the emphasis and use examples taken from those parts of your background that are most relevant, adding more details than it is necessary to include in the CV itself.

Here are a few ways Daisy Martin might do this if she decides to stay with one version:

Jobs in a library or bookshop – describe the **library job, P.A. work, computing**.

Jobs needing teamwork – mention the **club joint activity, environment work, theatre group**.

Jobs in education – use the **environmental work for children, computing, theatre**, and **craft skills**.

Jobs in an office – concentrate on the **computing skills, filing (library work)** and **P.A. experience.**

Jobs in the media – emphasise the **video library skills, theatre work, computing** and **poster design.**

Jobs in sales – stress persuasive skills: the ability to **get items for the theatre, helpers for environment work** and the **people to create a joint craft activity**, plus **P.A. experience.**

Jobs in community work – use the **environment work, craft club** and **library experience.**

SUMMARY

1. When producing a CV, decide on the best way to present information and make sure you include duties, responsibilities and what you have contributed.

2. Using action words makes more impact than simply stating the title and main tasks of the job.

3. Group similar jobs or activities together to make them easier to read or reduce the length of a CV.

4. Check and amend your CV on a regular basis, so that it is always up to date.

5. When using the same CV, be selective about what to emphasise in your covering letters.

Application Forms

Much of the advice in the chapter on CVs applies here too.

Some forms are not well designed, so add an extra sheet if there isn't enough room for important details.

You should *not* have to send a CV as well, as the form should give you the chance to set out:

◆ the reasons why you want the job and would be good at it
◆ full details of your relevant skills and experience.

However, you may have too much complex information to repeat in the form for one section and may prefer to write 'see attached CV' and send a copy with your form. In these cases, first check that there is no instruction telling you not to include a CV.

PREPARATION

As you may not be able to get hold of a second form easily, take great care you do not spoil it in any way. First appearances are very important in the job application process.

- It is a good idea to photocopy the form you are sent and complete it as a draft first, or fill in the only copy using pencil.

- When you are absolutely sure that you are happy with the wording, spellings and how you use the space, copy your draft onto the form or go over the pencilled words in pen.

- If your writing is very bad, print your answers clearly instead. It is very hard to word process an application form unless you are sent one online that is designed for completion this way.

- Forms are often photocopied by the employer and handed round to other people to read or use at interview, so use **black** ink that will copy clearly.

- Check any words you do not understand in a dictionary (or the glossary in this book), rather than guess their meaning before writing your answer.

- Follow the instructions carefully and answer *all* the questions as it will look odd to leave gaps.

CONTENTS

Here are the main sections you will be asked to fill in, although they may be in a different order.

1. Position

- This is the job you are applying for. Use the same wording as in the advertisement and, if there is one, include a reference number.

- They may want to know where you saw the job.

2. Personal details

◆ As well as your name and address, you may be asked for other information, often on a separate sheet. This could include:
  – age
  – if you are married
  – date of birth
  – nationality
  – previous surnames
  – ethnic origin
  – national insurance number
  – disability
  – car owner (if driving is part of the job).

There are many laws related to employment. You may have to provide more personal information than in the past so that the employer can check there is no discrimination taking place.

It is also important that employers do not take on people who are not legally allowed to work here, so extra information may be needed for that reason too.

3. Education and training

◆ If the form does not divide up this section, they will expect to see the school, college, university or training department name, general address and the courses you took with dates. With good results, add the grades you gained and the dates of exams.

◆ Include any courses you are taking now or plan to take in the future, even though you will have no certificate or award as yet.

EDUCATION			
School/college/ university attended	Qualifications	Date passed	Grade
Westfield College of Technology, Hull	City & Guilds car mechanics course	Finishes February 200X	

- ◆ If you gained extra skills outside the education sector, add these *somewhere* on the form (e.g. under *Leisure* or *Other*), or in your covering letter.

- ◆ Do not worry if you are not sure a course is 'Education' or 'Training' – just put it in, in the right date order, where there is room.

4. Employment

- ◆ Make sure you add the tasks or responsibilities of any job and use action words. (See details in Chapter 6.)

- ◆ Apart from your current post, choose the order that emphasises your relevant work experience, unless asked for 'most recent post first'.

- ◆ Reasons for leaving (but see later for help on answering awkward questions). If you are asked this question:
  - keep your answers brief
  - be positive
  - do not criticise or run down people or past jobs as it will reflect badly on you.
  - if you prefer, try not answering – this alone will not lose you an interview.

Here are a few examples of wording you could use:

I wanted to use my... skills more

I wanted to learn more about...

I wanted wider experience of...

My next job offered a better chance of (promotion, travel, managing other people, using my initiative, running my own...)

5. Leisure

As with the CV, only include activities that show you as successful, that you have organising skills, have a different range of skills or can work in a team, etc. (see previous chapter for details).

6. Reasons for applying

(This may be worded differently, e.g. *Relevant Experience and Skills* or *Additional Information*).

◆ This is the **most important part** of your form as it is what will 'sell' you. If there is not enough room or the question is missing, add extra sheets or put the answer in your covering letter.

◆ You may want to start with a short statement of interest.

◆ Do not be afraid to repeat information already included. It will be re-worded in this section to show you have the relevant skills, experience and interests.

◆ Group aspects of your life together under subheadings if possible, as these can be easier to read. (This is similar to the first part of a skills-based CV as described in the previous chapter.)

Example
I believe I have the relevant background to be successful as a Volunteer Organiser and would very much enjoy working in this field.

<u>Community Work</u>
My experience includes working as a helper at the local drop-in centre for over 10 years, and looking after an elderly relative since 1999. I also answer the phone at the Age Concern office once a month. From 1996 to 2000 I was a school governor.

<u>Driving</u>
I have my own car and full, clean driving licence. Last year I took a short course in car maintenance at the local college.

<u>Organising Skills</u>
When I first moved here, there was no library service at the hospital. I set up 'Library Friends' and organised a rota of retired people to take round a trolley of books twice a week.

THOSE DIFFICULT QUESTIONS
Unlike a letter and CV, application forms are designed by the employer and may include questions you would rather avoid.

If you tell lies on your application form and it is later discovered, you could lose your job.

Most of the awkward questions will be raised with your current or a recent employer, when they give you a reference, and so you may be unable to get away with ignoring them or not filling them in fully.

To answer the questions truthfully, but still be selected for an interview, it can help to understand why they are included.

Health

Any employer wants to feel you will carry out your job responsibly, and not be away sick for much of the time.

If you have had a long illness, a poor attendance record at work or have a condition that needs constant medication, reassure the employer that you can still do the job. For example:

Two years ago I suffered from stress and spent a month off work. The condition is now completely under control and I have carried out all my current duties without any problem.

Age

Although anti-age discrimination legislation comes into effect from October 2006 and you will find this question is rarely asked, before that date or if applying to companies or for jobs where the law does not apply, you need to think about the answers you give.

In these cases, as long as all the information you provide shows you can do the job and would do it well, do not assume that every employer is prejudiced and is going to discriminate against you just because of your age.

Here are some of the genuine reasons why your age might be a cause of concern to an employer:

- you may be very experienced or well qualified and so would expect a higher salary

- you may be near retirement age and so some long-term job training might be wasted

- you may be physically more frail than a younger person

- you will have less time to progress through the company over the years of your employment

- you may be much older than your work colleagues and may not fit in.

If you feel that any of these issues may be in their minds, try to counter them by stressing the positive side. For example, to avoid prejudice about physical abilities, indicate somewhere on the form how fit, active and healthy you are. For example:

Boxtree Hotel, Windermere
*Receptionist – taking room bookings, answering queries and organising bills. **Also help run children's activity clubs during the summer.***

Or:

Sports: Regularly play tennis or go swimming with family and friends.

Remember that there are so many cases where your maturity and experience will be of benefit, just make sure these are emphasised in your application.

Gaps

Taking time out to travel or to try starting your own business are perfectly acceptable reasons for gaps and should always be mentioned in an application form. However, don't forget to word any entry in a way that shows you in the best light.

Employers will normally fear that, apart from illness, a long gap that is not accounted for means you were in prison or cannot hold down a job and may be unreliable as an employee.

Criminal record

Any custodial sentence longer than $2\frac{1}{2}$ years must be declared. If getting a job because of your record seems very hard, try to apply to employers with good equal opportunities policies.

Criminal checks are now carried out if you want to work in a number of areas such as with children, the elderly, the chronically sick or many jobs which involve the law or have some form of legal protection, e.g. police, traffic wardens, nursing or accountancy, etc.

Short periods in prison or minor offences may be regarded as 'spent' after a fixed number of years. In these cases only, you can put 'none' if asked about a criminal record.

Help and advice are available from three organisations:

1. The Probation Service at www.probation.homeoffice. gov.uk.

2. NACRO (National Association for the Care and Resettlement of Offenders) who have a main website at www.nacro.org.uk or an information site at www.resettlement.info. You can phone them on 020 7840 6464 or send an email query to helpline@ nacro.org.uk.

3. The Apex Charitable Trust at St Alphage House, Wingate Annexe, 2 Fore Street, London EC2Y 5DA. Tel: 020 7638 5931, or on the Web at www.apextrust. com.

If it is not possible to get advice, try to word your answer in a positive way.

♦ Emphasise your achievements since your conviction.

♦ Mention any circumstances, e.g. personal problems, that influenced your behaviour but which no longer apply.

♦ Stress if your conviction was a long time ago.

♦ Show you have learned from the experience.

♦ Reassure them that it will not reoccur.

For example: *nine months in HMS Wellington for reckless driving, when suffering a period of depression following the breakdown of my marriage. I have never been in any trouble since. During that time, I started a brick-laying course and completed my HND in 2002.*

Unemployment

If you were out of work for a period of time, try to describe *any* activity that shows you:

- gained work-related skills, e.g. voluntary work in a charity shop

- studied, e.g. attending a day or evening class, teaching yourself a skill or taking an online course

- did something in the community, e.g. helping with a children's club or old people's centre or tidying up the environment, etc.

Either put the details in the *Work experience* section in the right place by date, or add to the *Leisure, Education* or *Other information* section.

If you are unemployed *now*, take up one or more of these activities so you have something to mention in your current applications.

Bringing up a family or caring for someone

Put this information in the work experience section by date and make sure you add any work-related or educational activities you were involved in during that time. For example:

2001–2005   Caring for a family member. During that time I supplied home-made cakes to the school shop and passed the computing course BBC Web-wise.

(See also Chapter 6 for alternative ways of wording this section.)

Reasons for leaving

Sacked

If you were sacked, future employers will be nervous about your honesty or reliability. If you are sure it will come out in your references, try to explain things from your point of view in a positive way, perhaps showing how you have overcome an earlier problem. For example:

When I sold my car and had to rely on a poor bus service I had trouble being punctual. I have now bought a motorbike and have never been late for my present job.

Made redundant

Word your answer to show that it was to do with changes in the organisation, not your own skills or abilities that were the cause. For example:

My department was reorganised as they decided to close the research laboratories to save money.

Retired

As you are now applying for a job, you may like to provide a more positive reason. You could say you left 'to change direction and work in...', 'to have more time to...' or 'make more use of my... skills or experience'.

Current salary

Many jobs, e.g. in the public sector, have an open, graded pay scale so that it is clear what the salary is for any position. For other types of work, it is up to the employer to pay what they think you are worth. They may ask for your current salary so that they can pay as little extra as possible.

If the question is asked on a form, try one of these strategies:

♦ Do not answer the question – leave it until you are in the interview.

♦ Tell them the 'package' (to include bonuses, etc.) rather than the basic salary, to show your income in the best light.

♦ Add a comment about why it is low to explain that you are worth more now. For example, you may have taken a low-paid job:
  – for the experience
  – to be in a certain area for personal reasons
  – to learn new skills
  – as the start of a new career, etc.

♦ If you are worried that you will be seen as too expensive, give the lowest figure without any extras and/or indicate you are more interested in the job itself than the pay.

FINAL WORDS

Make sure you take a photocopy of the form, or make a note of your answers. You will need to read through what you have written before any interviews. It will also save time when filling in other forms.

SUMMARY

1. Prepare your application form carefully as you may not be able to get hold of a second copy.

2. Answer all the questions, as gaps will be obvious.

3. Application forms ask tricky questions, but understanding the employer's concerns can help complete these in a positive way.

4. Keep a copy, to read through before interviews and to save time working out answers to the same questions when filling in other forms.

Online Applications

If you have access to a computer, you can now apply directly for some jobs. Many employers as well as the vacancy websites offer a link to an online form that you can fill in and send off straight away.

TAKE CARE!

Once your application has been sent, it will be too late to check for spelling mistakes, the wrong information or missing entries. It is therefore not a good idea to act rashly.

PRACTISE

Having opened the form on screen, disconnect from the Internet or save the form onto your own machine or a floppy disc. You can now practise answering the questions 'offline' in your own time.

For a word-processed form that has complex boxes and formats, copy the questions into a word-processing application as follows:

1. Select the whole form.
2. Click **Copy**.
3. Open your word-processing program.
4. Open the **Edit** menu and select **Paste Special.** This will allow you to copy a simpler version (e.g. Formatted or

Unformatted Text) that you can work with more easily.

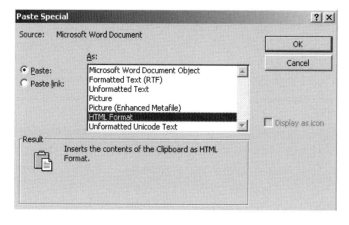

If you are in a library or college, print out a copy of the form and take it away to practise filling in – either create a word-processed document for your answers or write them out on paper.

Paste or copy the answers

When you have prepared your answers to each question using a word-processor, check very carefully for spelling mistakes and proofread to make sure it all makes sense.

You can now copy and paste the correct block of text into each section of the form if you want to send it in online. Do not use 'fancy' formats but keep to plain text as this will be easier to paste in.

1. Open your text file and select the correct block of text with the mouse.

2. Right-click and select **Copy** or go to **Edit – Copy**.

3. Re-open the form and click in the correct box.

4. Right-click and select **Paste** 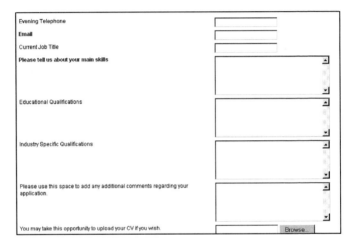.

5. Use the up and down arrows in the boxes to check through the entry and make sure it has copied correctly.

If you cannot copy and paste, type the answers carefully into the form from your notes.

Send your CV direct

There may be the chance on the same website to send in a copy of your CV. Click the **Browse** or **Upload** button to find the file on your machine, on a floppy disc in the (A:) drive or CD in the (D:) drive. Select the filename and press **Enter** and it will be sent direct to the website.

EMAIL

When you have completed a word-processed form or prepared a CV and covering letter, you may be able to send them via email. Either attach them as separate files or copy the contents into the main message window.

Note: Web-based accounts such as Hotmail and Yahoo! may be viewed with suspicion by some employers. If you have such an account, make sure the subject box of the email shows clearly that you are applying for an advertised vacancy or writing speculatively.

Attaching files to emails

Send files as email attachments if they are set out and formatted very carefully. Most employers should be able to open documents created using the latest version of Microsoft Word, but you can save them as simpler Rich Text Files (RTF format) to make sure.

1. With your message open, click the button labelled **Attach** or go to **Insert – File Attachment.**

2. Look through your computer files for the form or CV you want to send. For a web-based system, take your CV in on disc and look for it, e.g. on 3½ floppy (A:) for a floppy disc or D: if saved on a CD.

3. Click its name in the window and then click the Attach button.

4. It will now appear in an extra box, as a label next to the message or as a small picture in the main message window.

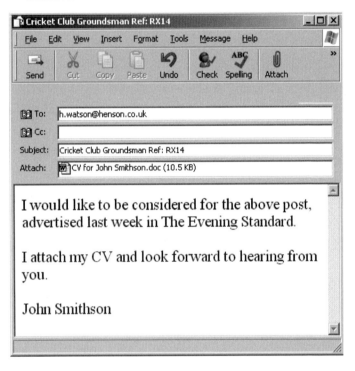

5. Use the body of the message to explain briefly why you are writing, if the application form or CV is sent as an attachment. If you are not including a covering letter, don't forget to outline your skills and reasons for applying in the message box if it would otherwise not be clear.

6. Complete all the boxes and send the email as normal.

Copying text

1. Copy and paste text into the body of the message if

you only want the recruiter to read the text and/or you worry that they will not accept attached files.

2. Make sure the subject of the message is the job title and any reference number.

DOWNLOADING

Employers may offer you a form to download that is not in a word-processed format but is a PDF file. This protects the layout and appearance and you will not be able to fill it in online. Instead, print out a copy to complete by hand.

To read a PDF file, you need the free program known as Adobe Acrobat Reader. Download and install the program first if it is not already on your machine. You should find a link to www.adobe.com on the same page as the form (although  no link will be offered if you are sent a form by email). Then, when you open the PDF file it will open straight into the reader.

KEEP A COPY

When you have the choice of sending forms online or by post, select your preferred method. If the form has to be signed, for example, printing it out may be the only option.

Whichever method you use, *always* keep a copy of your answers in some form, so you can refer to them before an interview.

EXTRA HELP

The point of a job application is to get an interview. If this is not happening, seek advice from a Next Step adviser or job centre. Take along copies of the job advertisements, your letters, CV and a completed application form and get advice on how they could be improved.

SUMMARY

1. Take care with online applications as it will be too late to correct mistakes if you send them off before checking.

2. When sending information by email, follow the steps to attach your documents safely.

3. If you are not being offered any interviews, take your application forms, CV or covering letters to a careers specialist who may be able to help you improve them.

9

Convincing at Interview

You might think that, having shown you have the skills and a strong interest in the work, there is nothing more for an employer to find out. But several factors are not visible from a paper application.

WHAT EMPLOYERS ARE LOOKING FOR

Will you fit in?
You may look good on paper, but will people get on with you and want you in the same office/store/department? This is where your appearance, way of speaking or attitude to the work may let you down.

Can you do what you say you can do?
For example, some people have a maths certificate and say they can handle money but, when asked to do a simple sum, show they do not have good enough numeracy skills.

You should be told if you will need to take any tests, e.g. typing or shorthand or give a short presentation. This is a common way for an employer to check out your skills.

Can you do what is needed?
If the job involves public speaking or answering the telephone, for example, your voice may be too faint or hesitant to be heard.

Do you really want the work?

Once it is explained in more detail, it may turn out you would not be happy in the job at all, or had the wrong idea about what was involved.

Do your capabilities or experience match what you put in your application?

An interviewer soon picks out people who have exaggerated or lied about their skills or knowledge.

Can they give you what you want?

You may ask about career prospects, travel, training or other factors that you want from the job but which are not on offer.

HOW INTERVIEWS WORK

Most interviews follow a similar pattern:

◆ welcome
◆ settling in, e.g. being asked about your journey, how easy it was to find the room, and being introduced to the interviewers
◆ being given a brief description of the company and/or job you are applying for
◆ questions about your experience
◆ questions about your educational background
◆ checking out how you see the job, what contribution you can make and how you might go about solving any problems
◆ questions about you as a person, including your leisure interests
◆ time for you to ask questions
◆ finish.

Rating

In many cases, interviewers use a marking scheme: e.g. for each area of questioning they may mark you as outstanding, above average, average, below average or unacceptable; or they will give you a grade from A to E.

This is meant to ensure that interviews are fair, as challenges to the results can be checked against the marking. Also, if you are seen by more than one person, it may be easier for them to come to an agreement on how you rate.

Most interviews cover similar ground – either the categories will be based around the job description or will cover more general areas such as social skills, motivation, appearance and personal qualities.

If you understand this, it may be possible for you to concentrate your preparation on areas where you think you are weakest.

PREPARATION

◆ As well as the job details, read your covering letter and CV or application form before you attend the interview. You need to know what you said!

◆ Remind yourself of the evidence you can offer for all your skills and experience. You will then be able to recall an example of when you used a skill or how you gained relevant experience.

◆ Try to get hold of material that tells you more about the employer or work sector and any news about them or a competitor, e.g. in

- company brochures
- house magazines
- websites
- trade journals
- local or national newspapers.

Tests

Some employers like to use aptitude or personality tests (referred to as psychometric tests) but you should be warned if these are part of the selection process. They are hard to prepare for, so it is best to relax and be yourself.

Aptitude tests are not the same as tests for practical skills such as typing as they look at the speed and accuracy of your verbal or numerical skills in general. Just work as quickly and carefully as you can and try to answer all the questions.

Personality tests often consist of a series of questions you must rate, e.g. on a scale from 1 to 5 or ranging from 'strongly agree' to 'strongly disagree'. For example:

I enjoy meeting people
I like working on my own

Or there may be multiple-choice questions. For each group of questions, you are asked to pick the answer nearest to or furthest from your way of thinking or working. For example:

Pick out the most and least typical from these four statements:
I am the sort of person who:

1. *Has lots of new ideas*   *Most: 1 2 3 or 4*
2. *Stays calm in a crisis*   *Least: 1 2 3 or 4*
3. *Is talkative*
4. *Has a wide circle of friends*

The results are worked out using a formula and are meant to predict whether you have the right personality for the job.

To try some of these questions, see *Passing Psychometric Tests* by Andrea Shavick (How To Books, 2002) or go to a website such as www.analyzemycareer.com or www.peoplemaps.co.uk.

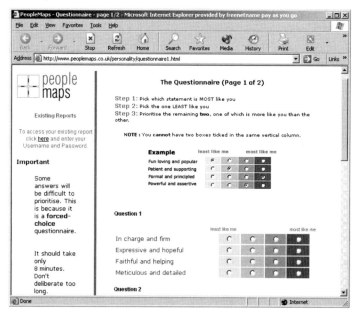

Arrival

To make a good impression, it is vital that you are on time. Check the journey you will need to take and have an alternative route, e.g. if your car does not start. Plan to arrive 10 minutes early – allow for a late bus, getting lost or dealing with a dripping umbrella.

Can you carry a mobile phone, the name of the recruiter and the company number? If held up by traffic or an accident, phone to apologise and they may rearrange the interview time.

Appearance

It is always best to look neat, clean and tidy even if the job is with an 'informal' organisation. It may be necessary to wear a suit. If you know you will have to wear a suit every day in the job, you have seen other people doing the job in suits or you would be working in a formal way or with the public, it is safest to wear one. (If you get it wrong, would you rather be *over*-dressed or *under*-dressed?)

Some employers do not like studs, earrings, long hair or beards. Decide if you want the job enough to remove or change yours.

Entrance and behaviour

You will usually have to wait your turn and then be collected from a reception area. Interviews are normally conducted by one, two or a panel of people and can last from 20 minutes to 1 hour.

It is very rare to take any documents with you to an interview (unless they have asked to see certificates or other official papers). An exception is a portfolio of artwork. When you go in, you may be offered a chair in the middle of the room or behind a desk or table.

- Shake hands if they offer this, but don't make a point of it if they stay seated. (Can you check out your handshake with a friend or relative? If it is limp or too firm, practice improving it.)

- Put any bags down neatly by your feet, but leave anything other than a handbag in reception if possible.

- In general, it is best to face the person who speaks to you and answer them directly, as it is very hard to 'speak to the group' when there is more than one interviewer. But if you can, briefly glance at other people in the room now and again and try to 'draw them in'.

- Keep eye contact with each interviewer and check their reaction. If they look bored or cross, finish the point you are making.

- When asked a difficult question, it is quite acceptable to pause for a short time to think about your answer.

- Remember that non-verbal signals will be given out by you and the interviewer, e.g. scratching, fidgeting, etc., so control your own and read theirs.

- Try very hard to show enthusiasm for the job – no one wants an unwilling employee.

- At the end, smile. Thank them for seeing you and try to leave without fuss.

Longer visits

Sometimes, you will be asked to arrive well before your interview or to stay on afterwards. The employer may offer you lunch or tea, or take you on a tour of the organisation.

In many companies or educational establishments, your tour guides may be junior members of staff or students.

Beware: As long as you are on the premises, you are being assessed. Do not ask silly questions, make rude remarks or behave in any way that would let yourself down. People at the lunch table, in reception or who take you round, are likely to be asked to report back. They will comment on how you behaved, what questions you asked and how much interest you showed in the organisation.

AWKWARD QUESTIONS

Don't be thrown by the questions you will be asked. Prepare answers in advance. Here are some of the commonest questions you are likely to face:

1. Tell us something about yourself
- ◆ **What they want**: A short summary of how you got to this point in your life and some of the choices you made. For example:

  I was born in Jamaica and came to Britain in the 1960s. After training as a house painter, I joined my present company where I have been running the paint store for the past two years.

- ◆ **What they don't want**: A long, rambling story about your early life or a launch straight into 'why I can do this job.'

2. Why should we give you the job? (Or what can you offer/ what are your strengths?)

- **What they want**: The points you made in your skills-based CV, application form under 'reasons for applying' or 'key skills', or in the main part of your covering letter. They also want to hear about any special personal qualities you can offer. For example:

  I have been working with children for the past three years and would really enjoy teaching them drama. As you know, I am a member of the local drama club and so I feel I have all the necessary skills to be successful in this post.

- **What they don't want**: Boasting or statements about 'how good you are' without the evidence.

3. What do you do in your spare time?

- **What they want**: To see balance, enthusiasm and to hear about one of your hobbies or interests explained in a little more detail. Try to show achievement, leadership, social skills, etc. If you can, pick one that links with a skill or interest needed in the job. If you don't have any interests, develop one quickly! For example:

  I have always enjoyed swimming, and a few years ago I took up diving. I now help run the local diving club and will be taking a small group of beginners on a trip to Greece next summer.

- **What they don't want**: To hear that you just sit in your room playing PC games or surfing the Internet, go to the pub or watch TV. 'Socialising with friends' is also not of interest.

4. What is your main weakness?

◆ **What they want**: To hear that you know yourself and can be honest, but don't have any major problems. It is best to mention lack of skills or knowledge, or think of something that could *also* be a strength. If you can, mention a weakness that you are overcoming. For example:

I don't know enough about networked computers and I often have to ask the IT helpdesk to sort out problems. That is why I decided to attend a PC evening course.

◆ **What they don't want**: You to list weaknesses that would make you a poor employee, e.g. lazy, always late, lose your temper easily, etc.

5. What do you know about us?

◆ **What they want**: To know that you have found out their main products or services and that you seem to understand their business.

You are one of the few local book clubs that cater for children. You have a very successful magazine which includes reviews of books written by children. I imagine your club is very popular with parents as it groups books into different age bands.

◆ **What they don't want**: To feel that you have done no research into them or their products or services.

6. Why do you want to work for us? (Or why do you want this job?)

◆ **What they want**: To see that you know something about their organisation and the work they are offering. Your answer should show how motivated you are, what positive things you can say about them and what you can bring to the job. For example:

As you know, I spend most of my spare time fishing. I want to work in a job where my knowledge of fishing would be useful. Yours is the largest fishing accessories shop in the area, with a good reputation, and so this job seemed just right for me.

♦ **What they don't want**: Too much interest in the perks of the job.

7. What do you think are the main aspects of this job?
♦ **What they want**: An answer that shows you know what the job will involve, and that you are aware of any special features. For example:

I know that a courier normally spends a lot of time sorting out people's problems and making sure clients enjoy their holiday. As this is a new area for your company, I imagine that I would also visit all the hotels on a regular basis to get to know the staff and build a good relationship with them.

♦ **What they don't want**: To hear a description of the wrong job or a stress on factors that are not part of this particular job.

8. Why are you leaving your present job?
♦ **What they want**: A positive statement that shows what you can offer, as well as what you want in your work, and that you have some ambition to succeed. For example:

Although I have enjoyed the work, I didn't find much scope for using any organisational skills. I decided to look for a job with a larger company where I would have an opportunity to take on more responsibility.

- **What they don't want**: A list of what was wrong with your last employer, the staff or working conditions.

9. What other companies/types of work are you considering?

- **What they want**: A picture of a logical search for jobs that offer similar types of work or the chance to use similar skills. For example:

As well as repairing musical instruments, I have been looking at jobs for people with skills in woodwork and carpentry in general.

- **What they don't want**: A mix of different types of job, as this could show that you don't have a clear idea of what you want to do.

10. What contribution did you make in your last job, or what was your major achievement?

- **What they want**: To find out more about what you can do for *their* organisation. Did you set up something new? Solve a problem? Overcome a barrier? Out-perform other people? If possible, think of something relevant to the job you are applying for. It does not have to be anything major.

If you had a low level job and did not contribute anything, it is better to describe something from your personal life than say there was nothing.

This wasn't at work, but I did set up a new craft club locally which has proved so successful we are now over-subscribed.

◆ **What they don't want**: To hear there was nothing.

11. What salary do you think you are worth/are you expecting?
◆ **What they want**: To pay as little as they can.

Make sure you find out the normal rate for this type of job and mention a range around that figure, unless you can justify more (or are overqualified and need to show you are not too expensive for them).

12. How will you cope working with younger people/having a manager who is younger than you?

◆ **What they want**: For you to allay their fears that you will not fit in.

There are two different answers you can give:

1. Describe any situations where you worked, studied or spent leisure time alongside younger people and had no problems.

2. Indicate that it is the personal qualities of your colleagues or supervisor that will matter to you (e.g. fairness, helpfulness, sense of humour, etc.) rather than their age.

Finally, for every job there will be job-specific questions related to the particular problems you may face or have to solve during your working day. For example, *How would you deal with difficult students in a college; cope with a distressed client in a medical centre; handle complaints from an irate customer; or sort out a piece of equipment that breaks down?*

Think about likely day-to-day problems that may occur so that you will be ready with a suitable answer.

MORE HELP

Many of the websites already featured in this book offering vacancy information or careers advice have sections offering tips on interview techniques. Try:

www.alec.co.uk

www.dsinteractive.com/selection/intqs.htm

www.ivillage.co.uk/workcareer/findjob

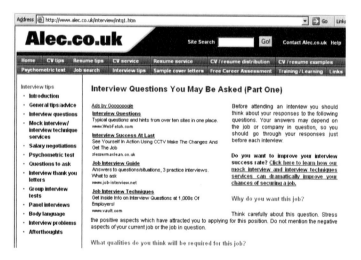

Finally, you can also buy more serious interactive CD-ROMs that take you through the interview process in some depth. *Teaching You Job Interview Skills* is one by Focus Multimedia – full details at www.focusmm.co.uk.

TWO-WAY PROCESS

The interview is not just about an employer checking that they want you. It is your chance to find out if you want the job.

Do you have any questions?

There should always be a chance to ask questions. Wait until the end of the interview, in case some of your questions are answered as you go through.

Here are a few things you really need to know:

- Where you will work.
- The hours, if not full time.
- When you start.
- What your main tasks will be.
- What support you will get.
- What training is provided.
- Chances of promotion or developing your career.

If you feel confident, you could try more personal questions such as:

- Can you describe a typical day?
- What has happened to people who have had this job before?
- What are the best things about working here?

Nothing to ask?

If you reach the end of the interview and everything has been covered, you may have no questions. Here are a few tips on how to say something.

- Ask if they can tell you 'a little more about.'
  - training
  - job tasks
  - contacts, e.g. with customers, other staff, patients, etc.
  - the structure of your new department
  - the company itself (products, services or how it is doing).

- Ask when you will hear the results of the interview.

If you must:

- ask about the starting salary (but take care not to get into an argument at this stage!)

- say they seem to have answered all your questions during the interview.

Don't ask too many questions about what you will get out of them in terms of perks. Leave the interviewers with a positive image.

OVER THE TELEPHONE

For some jobs such as market research, customer services, call centres, help desks, sales, interviewing or distance learning tutoring, much of your time may be spent talking to people over the phone. Employers will therefore often want to carry out a telephone interview for these types of work to check on your voice, manner and how you handle yourself.

Also, if you have applied speculatively and follow up your letter with a phone call, you may end up being quizzed on the spot. These are all still interviews, so you should prepare in exactly the same way as you would for one that is face to face.

Time and place

If it is possible, agree a day and time for the interview so you can make sure that you will have a quiet room to yourself.

Content of the interview

This will probably follow a similar pattern to a normal, face-to-face interview. There may be two people sharing a phone link or just a single interviewer, and you will be asked questions about your past experience, skills and attitude to the work.

With this type of interview, you can have your CV and other reference material with you if you need to refer to dates or details in your background, and this may help you feel more relaxed. Instead of worrying about how you look, concentrate on sounding warm and friendly, and speak clearly at all times. Don't forget to ask for the name and contact details of the interviewer in case you want to check on anything later.

One tip is to have a notepad handy so you can jot down ideas as they occur (in case you have a chance to feed extra information in before the end of the interview) and write up a note straight after it ends. In particular, remind yourself of any difficult questions so you are better prepared for future interviews.

AFTER AN INTERVIEW

It is hard to wait for the results of an interview. If you do not hear soon, it may be because people are away, the letter got lost in the post or details need to be finalised. But this is not common.

More likely, they have changed their minds about their needs and need to reorganise things, or they have offered the job to another candidate and are waiting for him/her to accept. If the offer is turned down, they may come back to you with an offer later.

Should you hurry them?

◆ **If you were told you would hear very soon**: wait at least five working days and then contact the Personnel Department or your interviewer to ask when you will hear from them.

◆ **If you were not given a time**: wait at least eight working days before making contact.

◆ **In general**: do not to write or phone to say thank you or to provide extra information (unless it is of vital importance or they asked you for it) but try to be patient for a few days.

SUMMARY

1. Prepare carefully for interviews so you are not caught out on the day.

2. Some questions always seem to come up, so think up answers well in advance.

3. Your arrival, appearance and behaviour during the interview are all important aspects to consider.

4. Even when outside the interview room, you are still being assessed.

5. Remember that an interview is a two-way process. You must find out if you want the job as well as convince an employer that they should employ you.

6. Some interviews may be conducted over the telephone, but prepare for them in the same way as more usual interviews.

7. Waiting for the results can be hard, but it is best to be patient.

(10)

Should You Take the Job?

It can be so wonderful to be offered a job that you may say *yes* too quickly. Try to make your decision *before* they phone. After an interview, pretend you are offered the job. How do you feel?

- ◆ Over the moon.
- ◆ Quite pleased.
- ◆ Anxious.
- ◆ Disappointed.

OVER THE MOON
You should accept: If the job sounded perfect or even better than you hoped, and all the conditions were right.

Hesitate: if you didn't find out enough about some of the key features.

Make a list of questions to ask before making a final decision.

QUITE PLEASED
Think about the factors that made this a not-quite-ideal job. Are they going to stop you enjoying the work or looking forward to joining the organisation?

One method is to divide the job into **Pros** and **Cons**.

Pros	Cons
Salary better than hoped	Long journey to work
Nice canteen	Boss wasn't very nice
Other staff friendly	Parts of the work seem boring
Easy tasks	Have to learn to use new photocopying equipment that looks tricky
Management responsibilities	
In work before Christmas	

As well as the length of each column, how important is each point? You should find that setting out pros and cons helps you get a better sense of whether the job is right for you or not.

Negotiate

For some jobs, it may be possible to agree some changes with the employer that would make the job more attractive. For example, they may accept different start or end times, part-time work or a job share, or give you different duties to make more use of your experience.

It is also quite reasonable to try to agree an increase in the salary if you believe it is too low and you have special skills or experience to offer.

The best time to try to get a better deal is at the same time that they offer you the post.

ANXIOUS

This means there are some serious things wrong with the job. If there is one factor that is of major concern, try to sort it out. Do you need to talk to family members, or get in touch with the company?

You may prefer to wait until they offer you the job, but make sure you raise it straight away and get clear answers before accepting or rejecting the offer.

DISAPPOINTED

When the job is not what you hoped, but not so bad that you would reject it instantly, it is hard to know how to react.

Consider these points:

- If you really need the work, and it is your first job offer for some time, it may be worth saying yes and giving it a go. It could improve.

- Looking for another job when you are in work, no matter how unsatisfactory, is easier than when you are unemployed.

- If you know in your heart that you do not really want the job, it could save a lot of time and effort, and will allow another candidate to accept the job, if you say no.

KEEP GETTING REJECTED?

If you don't get a job offer, try to find out why. There are two main sources of help: the interviewer and yourself.

The interviewer

Ask for feedback. Someone should phone or write to you with comments about your performance.

If you find out that it was between you and another candidate, but they had more experience or better qualifications, be pleased that you almost got the job. In this case, suggest they keep your details on file and let you know if another vacancy arises that would be suitable.

If one or two employers say the same thing, e.g. you didn't seem keen or flexible enough, you can then work on this aspect before the next interview.

A pattern of rejections for work you can do is more worrying, especially if the employers do not say anything helpful in their feedback. In this case, you need to think back over your recent interviews.

Your own analysis

◆ Were there any questions you couldn't answer or felt uncomfortable about, or were you taken by surprise with the direction of the interview? Prepare for these more carefully before your next interview.

◆ Are you applying for the wrong jobs? It is possible that you have discovered you will need skills, experience or interests that you do not have or want to use, or that you are competing against people who are very different to yourself. Redirect your applications to other types of work or different employers.

◆ The wrong attitude? Were you too casual in dress or in your answers, or did you find it hard to show much enthusiasm? Either show more interest next time or read the signs and try for other jobs that would suit you better.

♦ Too nervous? Why not join a relaxation class at a local adult education centre?

EXTRA HELP

If nothing seems to work, it may be time to seek professional help. Go back to a careers service or job centre and try to find a course to go on or an adviser who can help you work on your interview skills.

ALTERNATIVE LIFESTYLES

Many people decide not to go through the job search process at all, or to change tack if it is not turning out to be very successful. Instead, they find an alternative way of earning a living. Here are a few suggestions.

Self-employment/starting your own business

If you have a skill or great interest in something, or have a good idea for a business – perhaps after spotting a gap in the market – other people may like to pay for your services or products. There may even be government grants to help you get started.

Freelance work is available in a wide range of work areas including proof-reading, copy-editing, programming, catering, accountancy, writing, web design, training, translating, book-keeping, PR and editing. To get started, identify a few organisations that employ such workers or may require your services and send a speculative letter and CV. You may also need to provide samples of your work and decide on rates of pay and an acceptable workload beforehand.

PRIME, a subsidiary of the charity Age Concern England, has helped hundreds of over-50s across the country make the move into starting up their own business or becoming self employed. View their details at www.primeinitiative.org.uk.

If you are completely new to the idea, another good starting point is your local Business Link – find them via the government's website at www.businesslink.gov.uk.

eBay

A new lifestyle that has grown with the Internet is selling second-hand goods on eBay – the auction website at

www.ebay.co.uk. You will make money if you sell goods for more than you spend on them, so start cooking or sewing, turn out the attic or visit car boot sales, flea markets or second-hand shops for things you could sell on the Web. One way to really earn money is to add value, e.g. by repairing broken or damaged crockery or furniture.

Read the general articles on selling available on the site before putting in your first advertisement.

Self-sufficiency

We mainly work to earn enough for rent, food, clothes, heating and light. If you have land, you can grow your own food and sell excess for other things you may need. Sometimes, a group of people living in this way join together to form a co-operative so that they can help each other and share ideas and equipment.

Visit the Co-operative Assistance Network at www.co-op-assist.co.uk for information sheets on this way of life.

Communes

Some people band together to set up self-sufficient communities based on religious or other beliefs. They have their own rules and leadership structure and can be quite strict, so make sure these are acceptable before you join.

There are many small websites set up by different communes, but you may like to start by visiting Diggers & Dreamers at www.diggersanddreamers.org.uk/. They have articles and a publication list on their site as well as vacancy lists for living or short-term volunteering.

Volunteering

Many jobs are available overseas or within the community that pay expenses and let you live and eat cheaply or even for free.

Warning: Some organisations want older people, but if you join a mainstream group of volunteers, remember that you may be much older than any of them, so decide if this would suit you.

Charities looking for mature volunteers include:

♦ Community Service Volunteers' Retired and Senior Volunteer Programme (RSVP), found at www.csv-rsvp.org.uk.

♦ REACH (at website www.volwork.org.uk).

♦ International postings are offered by i-to-i at www.i-to-i.com.

♦ Experience Corps, who have a website at www.experiencecorps.co.uk, want to use your skills and experience if you are 50–65.

♦ Don't forget the CAB. Many of the staff in Citizen's Advice Bureaux are volunteers and you should find it easy to locate your nearest bureau if you want to call in and find out what is involved.

A year out

Finally, if you want to travel, it can be a valuable experience to visit other countries for a year or so, taking odd jobs to earn enough for your food and accommodation. Most people who have done this have something more to offer when they come back in terms of experience, new languages or greater understanding of the world. It is an option that is just as valid for older people as college or school leavers, and may even help you decide on a different career path.

Find out about gap years at www.gapyearforgrownups. co.uk.

SUMMARY

1. Decide whether or not you want to take the job before it is actually offered.

2. Weigh up the pros and cons if you are not sure the job is right for you.

3. It may be better to take a job you are not keen on, rather than stay unemployed.

4. If you are not getting any job offers, find out why. If you can, get help with your interview skills.

5. Sometimes, a different way of life that does not involve working for an employer may be a better option.

Glossary of Job-hunting Terms

Like many activities, looking for a job has its own technical or specialist shorthand terms – jargon. As you search for jobs or make applications, you may come across these words in your reading and will need to understand and use them correctly. Here are some of the most common.

Chronological order Listing items such as jobs or educational courses in date order.

Commission-only pay Some jobs, for example in sales, only pay if you sell something. This means you have no basic salary to rely on.

Conscientious A personal quality shown by someone who takes care with their work, checks everything, finishes off jobs, arrives on time and is generally reliable and hardworking.

Curriculum vitae (CV) A document that sets out your personal details such as contact information, skills, past jobs and hobbies.

Discrimination If you are rejected because of your age, sex, ethnic origin or religion, this is known as discrimination. In most cases, this is now illegal or will soon become so.

File format When sending a CV or letter of application by email, you may be asked to provide your documents in a different format to make sure they can be opened. The most common are Word document files (DOC), Rich Text files (RTF) and plain text files (TXT).

Job description Details of the main duties of any job such as the tasks you must carry out and who you report to.

Motivation This shows how keen you are to take part in an activity or carry out a task, or how ambitious you may be in developing your career.

Office procedures Various tasks carried out in offices such as faxing, filing, word-processing letters and answering the phone.

Pro rata Part-time jobs may be shown as 0.5 or 0.75 FTE, i.e. as half or three-quarters of the hours worked by someone full time (FTE = Full Time Equivalent). Pro rata means the part-timer will get part of the salary, based on the number of hours they work. A salary of £18,000 pro rata when working 0.5 FTE will pay half, i.e. £9,000 per year.

Referees People who can confirm you carried out the work or gained the skills you put in your application. They normally include your most recent employer or a tutor if you have been in full-time study or on any training courses. The comments they make form a **reference**.

Search engine A website such as www.google.co.uk or www.gigablast.com that will help you find information on any topic you choose. The words you use as the basis for your search are known as 'key words'.

Shortlist Those people selected for an interview after all the applications have been considered.

Speculative application The approach you make to an employer to express an interest in working for them, even though you do not know if they have any vacancies at that time.

Transferable skills Many employers need you to be able to send emails, answer the phone, file documents or use a calculator. These are transferable skills as they are useful across a number of different jobs.

Work experience Any experience gained as part of your normal paid work, during time spent with an employer learning about jobs *or* when acting as an unpaid helper or volunteer.

Online help

For words not listed, don't forget that you can find help on the Web: visit one of the dictionary websites such as www.freedictionary.com to find a definition.

Appendix – Working with a Computer

INTERNET CONNECTION

If using a home-based computer, the type of connection that you have does not matter. It can be dial-up on a subscription basis (where you dial a free phone number and pay an agreed amount each month for 50–80 hours of use); pay as you go (you pay for each minute that you are online through your normal telephone bill); or broadband (a faster connection that is connected continuously and which allows you to use your telephone at the same time).

INTERNET SERVICE PROVIDERS

If you have just bought a new computer that does not have an Internet connection, you will need to choose from the huge variety of companies that provide this service, known as internet service providers (ISPs.) They all work in a similar way but you may need to consider these factors:

1. The type of connection you pay for depends on the amount of time you are likely to spend online. For very limited use, you may prefer pay as you go or to take out a 'light use' subscription. For heavier use, or if you think you will need to work with large files such as pictures or audio/video material, you may prefer a

'heavy use' subscription or to go for broadband.

2. ISPs vary in the services they offer but you can change from one to another if you feel you have made the wrong initial choice. In particular, look at the costs of their technical support (the help-desk); the quality of any customised indexes to a range of pages on entertainment, shopping, travel, etc.; whether they offer screening of inappropriate material; if there is enough space for your own web pages; and what access there is to different email accounts. In time, you will also discover if your ISP offers quick and reliable Internet connections and up-to-date services such as broadband or if it is time to move to another provider.

3. Discs containing all the programs needed for registering with an ISP are available in supermarkets, shops and on magazine covers. Once you have established a connection, search the Web for a replacement and you will be able to register and change over to a preferred ISP online.

SEARCHING THE WEB

Search engines

Everyone has their favourite website for locating information, and you will soon find you use just two or three for most searches. Here are a few you could try.

www.google.co.uk The main reasons for the popularity of this site are that there are no advertisements or annoying 'pop-up' windows to confuse you, and the searches seem to be intelligent so that you do not usually get offered nonsense sites when searching. New developments include good quality maps.

www.gigablast.com This site is fairly new and, like Google, is also free of advertisements.

www.ask.co.uk This is sometimes known as Ask Jeeves. You can type a full sentence into the search box if you are not sure which key words to use.

www.yahoo.co.uk This website offers both key word search and categories under which a limited number of relevant websites have been grouped, which can make searching more manageable. It also offers a free email service.

How to search

1. If necessary, connect to the Internet, or simply open the program that will allow you to view web pages by double-clicking the icon (small picture) link.

2. When the window opens:

If you know the name of the organisation:

a. In most cases, the web address will be:

www.**[name.]**co.uk or www.**[name.]**com

For example:
www.independent.co.uk (newspaper)
www.reed.co.uk (employment agency)
www.waitrose.com (supermarket)
www.hsbc.co.uk (bank)
www.microsoft.com (American computing company)
www.fish4jobs.co.uk (general job vacancies)

b. Click in the Address box, situated just below the toolbar buttons, type the new web address over the entry that is there and then press your **Enter** key or click the **Go** or **Search** button. (**Note**: You will see http:// added to the address but you do not need to type this in.)

c. Use the index or labels to click and open the page you want, or start using the boxes on screen to type in your search words.

If you don't know where to look:

d. Type the address for a search engine: e.g. www.google. co.uk or www.gigablast.com into the Address box and press **Enter**.

e. In the empty box on screen, type some key words or phrases.

e.g. Jobs in sales
Publishing companies in Nottingham
Training as an administrator

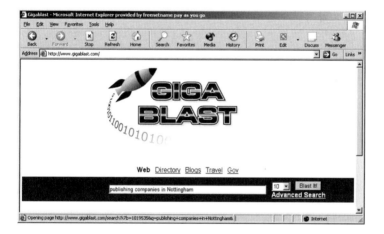

f. Check the button labelled 'pages from the UK' (on Google) or add 'UK' to your key words if you want to find only British information or organisations.

g. Press **Enter** or click the **Search** button (e.g. labelled *Blast it!*) on Gigablast.

h. When the list of websites appears, click any heading (it will be blue and underlined) to open that page and read the contents.

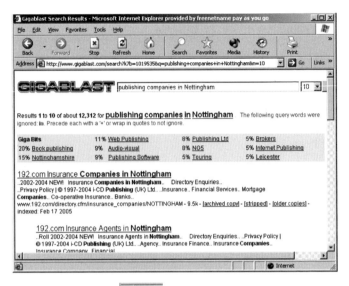

i. Click the **Back** button to return to the list at any time.

j. When you find the information you are looking for, either note it down or print out the page by clicking your **Print** 📖 button.

Directory search

Some search engines offer a different type of search based on a hierarchy of pages grouped under various headings. This is known as a directory search. Simply click the top-level heading and then click subsequent lower-level links until you come to a limited group of relevant web pages.

Your 'route' will be displayed on screen so that, if you come to a dead end, you can retrace your steps and take a slightly different direction. For example, a directory search of www.excite.co.uk through the categories *Business – Employment – Job Search – Interview Advice* displayed 35 possible sources of help.

Finding exact information

For any search, pages can be very wordy. To go quickly to the correct section, open your **Edit** menu and click **Find (on this page).** In the box, type your key words and click the **Find Next** button. This will take you to the first mention of the exact phrase on the page. Keep clicking the button to move through the document.

Bookmarking pages

During your searches, you will come across pages that you will want to revisit. To make a shortcut to the page, you must 'bookmark' it, i.e. add it to a menu of links. If using Internet Explorer, the menu is known as *Favorites*.

1. Click the star-shaped **Favorites** toolbar button or the menu and, when the folders list opens to the left of your screen, click **Add**.

2. Now select an appropriate folder from the *Create in* list in which to store the link, or click *New Folder* to create one specially. You can also amend the words in the **Name**: box if they are too long. Click OK to store the link.

3. Next time you want to open the page, click **Favorites** to display the list of folders, click the parent folder to open it and then click the page name. The page will immediately open on screen.

SETTING UP A WEB-BASED EMAIL ACCOUNT

Go to one of the many websites that offer free emails such as www.hotmail.co.uk, www.yahoo.co.uk, www.postmaster.co.uk or www.email2me.com.

Register by clicking the link and completing the form:

1. Decide how you want your address to appear. As you will be using email for a job search, avoid silly or pet names but stick to first name (or initial), surname and perhaps a special number. Have alternatives in mind in case your first choice is already taken.

2. Your full address with appear something like
jsherman45@hotmail.co.uk
or shermanj45@yahoo.co.uk

3. Choose an easy-to-remember (but not easy to guess) password combining upper and lower case letters and numbers. You will need to type it into the form twice as all you see are **** or •••• to prevent other people reading it on the screen.

4. Select a prompt from the questions, and type a truthful reply to help if you forget your password and the system needs to establish your identity. Examples include your primary school, mother's maiden name or favourite pet.

5. Only complete personal questions on the form if they are compulsory, and take off ticks in boxes offering newsletters or advertising.

6. Once your name (known as your username or ID) and password have been accepted, type them *both* into the log-in box when you visit the website, always keeping to the correct upper and lower case letters as passwords are case-sensitive.

WORD-PROCESSING

Opening Word

If you have the program icon on your desktop, double-click to open. Otherwise, find it from the **Start – All Programs** menu.

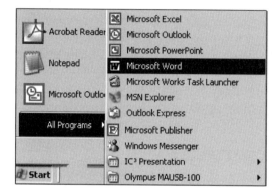

Creating a document

When the program opens, a blank document appears on screen. A black flashing vertical bar, the cursor, will show where your words will appear and you can start typing straight away.

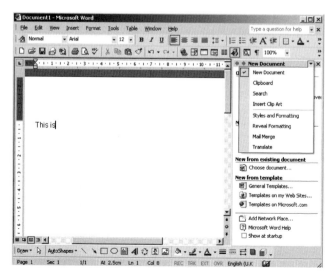

In Word 2002, an extra pane known as the Task Pane will appear as you work, offering shortcuts and guidance, but you can remove it at any time to give yourself more room by clicking the close button marked with an **X** in the top corner.

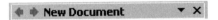

As your typing reaches the right-hand margin of the page, the next word will be moved automatically to the start of a new line by a process known as word wrap. There is no need to press **Enter** to move to the next line unless you are beginning a new paragraph.

Making changes
If you have carried out any typing before, you will know that the Backspace ⌫ and Delete 🔲 keys on your keyboard can be used to erase letters to the left or right of the cursor. You can also add extra text between letters or words by clicking on screen with the mouse and then typing the new entries where the cursor is flashing.

The program stores rules of grammar as well as a large dictionary, and if you break a rule or type a word that is not recognised, the words will be underlined with a wavy line – red for spelling and green for grammar. Use the right mouse button when clicking on the line and you will be offered alternative spellings and the chance to either ignore the error message or add the word to the dictionary.

Note: Once you have mastered the spell checker, it is all too easy to rely on it to pick up all errors. However, it will only pick out mis-spelt words, not words out of context. So, for example, a sentence such as '*I walked for the company for fifth years*' requires careful proof-reading.

Saving your work

To save important documents such as letters or CVs, save early by clicking the **Save** 💾 button on the toolbar soon after you start work. This opens the *Save As* window.

Each document has a generic name, e.g. *Document1*, until given your choice of filename, and can be saved in one of a number of locations. Click the arrow in the *Save in*: box to save:

♦ onto the hard disc of your computer, in the area set aside for files labelled *My Documents,* or a folder that has been created inside it

♦ on a floppy disc labelled 3½ Floppy (A:)

♦ on a CD in the D: or E: drive through a process known as writing or 'burning'.

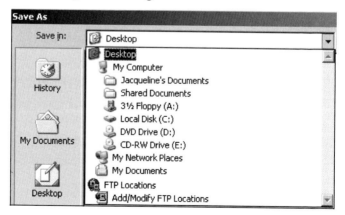

If you want to create a folder for all your job-seeking documents, click the **Create New Folder** 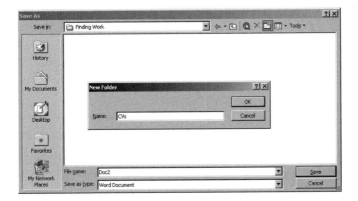 button. You can create sub-folders within folders to group specific files: first make sure the correct 'parent' folder is showing in the *Save in:* window.

After naming the new folder, check it appears in the *Save in:* window, change the document name in the *File name:* box and then click the **Save** button in the bottom, right-hand corner of the window.

Save As

When you are applying to a number of similar employers, you won't want to create each new letter from scratch but will need to change a few details. In this case, save subsequent versions of your original letter with a new name. Open the *Save As* box from the **File – Save As** menu and change the file name before clicking the Save button.

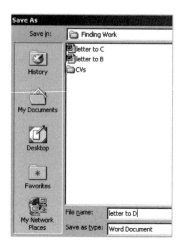

SAVING ONTO A CD

Many computers now come with CD-writers so that you can save your work onto an optical disc by 'burning' or writing it on. You can use a CD-R disc, which allows you to write to it only once, or a more expensive CD-RW that you can use for work you want to rewrite and save repeatedly. (Take care if you are using public computers, however, as some machines may not be able to read a CD-RW very easily.)

With Windows XP machines, simply place the disc into the writer. The CD Drive window will open and you can now locate the parent folder to find the work you want to save. Select it and use the Task Pane option to *Copy this file*.

When the *Copy Items* window opens, click the correct drive and then click the **Copy** button.

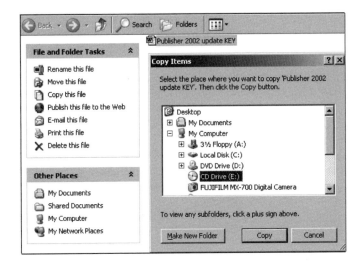

Return to the CD-Drive window and you will see a pale copy of the file. Click the *Write these files to CD* link.

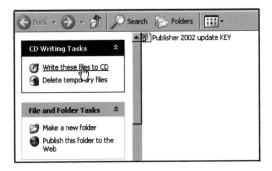

When the Wizard opens you have the chance to name the disc and then the file will be copied across. At the end, the disc will be ejected from the drive.

PRINTING A COPY

To print one copy of any document, click the **Print** button. If you want to print several copies, or selected pages of a long document, go to **File – Print** to open the dialog box and change any settings before clicking OK.

Index

advertise yourself, 47
age, 110
age limit, 27
Age Positive, 28
alternative lifestyle, 148
analyse an advert, 50
Apex Charitable Trust, 113
application forms, 104
aptitude tests, 128
Ask Jeeves, 159
attachments, 121

being rejected, 146
bookmark webpage, 163
browser, 6
burning onto CD, 170

careers service, 28
CD-R, 170
CD-RW, 170
Citizen's Advice Bureau, 151
commission, 153
company report, 54
company websites, 43

Connexions, 29
covering letter, 68
create new folder, 169
criminal record, 112
Curriculum Vitae (CV), 82
  by date, 92

dialog box, 172
Directgov, 23
directory, 162
disabilities, 23
discrimination, 2
downloading, 123

eBay, 149
email, 120
email alert, 34
employment agencies, 39
empty statements, 58
evidence, 60

Favorites, 163
file format, 153
Find on this page, 163
find out more, 53

find vacancies, 32
font, 83
freelancing, 148
Friends Reunited, 43
functional CV, 86

gaps explained, 112
gigablast, 159
Google, 158

health, 110
help, 124
hidden agenda, 51
home working, 38

I.D., 165
IAGP, 29
improve yourself, 21
institutes, 37
interests, 24
interim management, 38
Internet café, 5
interview appearance, 130
interview questions, 132
ISP, 157

jargon, 153
job description, 53
job centres, 44
journals, 36

Learn Direct, 22

length of a CV, 86
link letter to CV, 102
local newspapers, 34

magazines, 36
motivation, 24

NACRO, 113
national press, 35
negotiate, 145
networking, 46
New Deal 50 plus, 45
new mail message, 67
Next Step, 29

offered a job, 144
office procedures, 154
online applications, 118
organise job search, 6

password, 165
person specification, 54
personality tests, 128
post your CV, 34
prepare for interviews, 127
printing, 5
pro rata, 154
proof-reading, 168
pros and cons, 145
Prospects, 29
psychometric tests, 128

reasons for leaving, 115
redundant, 115
referees, 74
references, 74
register email account, 164
résumé, 82
retired, 115

sacked, 115
salary checker, 27
save, 168
Save As, 169
scams, 39
search engine, 158
search the Web, 158
send for details, 65
shop windows, 38
shortlist, 154
skills, 11
speculative letters, 76
spent criminal record, 112
start your own business,
    148

telephone interview, 140
training, 11
transferable skills, 17, 155

U3A, 23
unemployment, 114
URL, 44
username, 165

vacancy websites, 40
values, 25
volunteers, 151

web page address, 44
what employers look for,
    57
word-processing, 166
word wrap, 167
working conditions, 10
World Wide Web, 6

Yahoo!, 159
your questions, 139

If you want to know how … to be headhunted

'This book is intended to meet a pressing need. Every day, large numbers of people contact executive search firms in the hope of finding a job or a non-executive directorship. Many of them do so without fully understanding the business of headhunting. We looked for a book to help such candidates, without success – and therefore decided to write one of our own.'

John Purkiss and Barbara Edlmair

How to be Headhunted
The insider's guide to making executive search work for you
John Purkiss and Barbara Edlmair

If your looking for a senior executive position – or a seat on the board – this book will tell you what you need to know.

- Learn about the search industry and the prominent firms within it
- Understand the recruitment process and make it work to your advantage
- Prepare a persuasive covering letter and a 'head-hunter-friendly' CV

Headhunting has long been shrouded in mystique. This book is *the* insider's guide, packed with practical tips to help you approach executive search firms.

ISBN 1 85703 996 3

If you want to know how … to excel at psychometric and management tests

'The good news is there are thousands of brilliant firms out there offering everything from sky-high salaries, profit-related bonuses, long holidays, flexible working, staff discounts, free shares, free canteens, health and life insurance, advanced training, gyms, outings, holidays... not to mention the job satisfaction and level of responsibility you've always known you could handle. But the reality is that the days when all you needed to land a top job was a great CV and a sparkling performance at interview are long gone. Now you must also pass a whole range of psychometric and management tests with flying colours. And that's exactly what this book is here to help you to do.'

Andrea Shavick

Management Level Psychometric & Assessment Tests
Everything you need to help you land that senior job
Andrea Shavick

Whether you're after a junior management, senior management or even director level position, or simply want to familiarise yourself with the very latest selection and recruitment techniques this book will meet your needs. It includes:

- 35 genuine management level practice psychometric tests and a guide to online testing.
- Everything you need to know about personality questionnaires, plus loads of practice material.
- A complete guide to what to expect and how to survive an assessment centre visit.
- Detailed information on high-level assessment centre exercises commonly used to test candidates.
- A guide to researching your chosen organisation.

ISBN 1 84528 028 8

If you want to know how ... to pass psychometric tests

Over 95% of FTSE 100 companies use psychometric testing to select their staff; as do the police, the Civil Service, local authorities, the Armed Forces, the Fire Service, financial institutions, retail companies, the communications industry, the motor industry, the power industry – the list is endless. In fact, the vast majority of large–medium sized organisations use psychometric tests to recruit. So if you're looking for a job you need to know what to expect. This book gives you the information, confidence and practice to do that, and more.

Passing Psychometric Tests
Know what to expect and get the job you want
Andrea Shavick

'An insightful book.' – *The Guardian*

'A very good aid for those who might find themselves facing a psychometric questionnaire.' – *Irish Examiner*

ISBN 1 85703 819 3

If you want to know how ... to prepare for interviews

'It's the interviewer's prerogative to throw just about any question they can think of at the interviewee. So you might think that it's almost impossible to prepare for an interview. But the truth is that 80% of interview questions revolve around 20 common themes. And many inter-viewees let themselves down by not thinking about these themes, preparing and rehearsing responses to them.

'Many candidates then go on to create a wrong impression. Remember that an interviewer has to *like* you and warm to you as a person, as well as want to work with you because you answer the questions well. I see too many candidates who talk too much or come across as nervous or unfriendly. If you get the chance to rehearse with a friend and get some feedback on just how you come across, you will improve your chances no end.'

Rob Yeung

Successful Interviews – Every Time
Rob Yeung

'*Successful Interviews* is the type of book that one may not wish to share with others who are job seeking in competition with oneself. Nevertheless, I owe a debt of gratitude to Dr Rob Yeung for sharing his experiences with us...' – *S. Lewis, Coventry*

'This book is an invaluable source of information for job hunters on preparing for interviews, tests and assessment centres.' – *Jonathan Turpin, Chief Executive of job hunting website fish4jobs.co.uk*

ISBN 1 85703 978 5

How To Books are available through all good bookshops, or you can order direct from us through Grantham Book Services.

Tel: +44 (0)1476 541080
Fax: +44 (0)1476 541061
Email: orders@gbs.tbs-ltd.co.uk

Or via our website

www.howtobooks.co.uk

To order via any of these methods please quote the title(s) of the book(s) and your credit card number together with its expiry date.

For further information about our books and catalogue, please contact:

How To Books
3 Newtec Place
Magdalen Road
Oxford OX4 1RE

Visit our web site at

www.howtobooks.co.uk

Or you can contact us by email at info@howtobooks. co.uk